SACRIFICIED

© 2011

MARTON
PUBLISHING INTL
Words for the World

SACRIFICIED © 2011

Given to an Empire, found by God

By Tony Woods

(As told by Naoki Noguchi)

MARTON PUBLISHING INTL
Words for the World

Foreword

The first time I met Naoki Noguchi, he and an older missionary friend of mine, Bob Boatwright, were laughing and joking together about something. My Japanese wasn't good enough yet to follow along, but I knew then and there that I needed to get to know this man. He just seemed so real to me in a world that in every way was anything *but* real. I had brought my family to Japan and had been there long enough to conclude that the Japanese were unknowable. It wasn't just the language; everything about these people was so different, so *alien* from anything else I had ever experienced. We had been in language study for a little over a year, and had come to that "let's give it one more month before we chuck the whole thing" phase of our career which is common to most missionaries in this part of the world.

Bob Boatwright must have sensed my stress, and I'm sure by God's leading responded in the best way possible: he introduced me to Naoki and added, "We thought we might go skiing tomorrow; why don't you come along?"

I did, and the next day found me at a beautiful ski slope just west of the city of Sendai, in northern Japan. Truth be known, I wasn't that great a skier, but certainly didn't plan to admit to it. I didn't have to; the fact became obvious about five seconds after my skis hit the ground. Naoki and I were traveling up together on the chairlift, and when we disembarked, my skis took off with a mind of their own. In desperation, I clutched at the nearest thing in sight, which happened to be Naoki. We both went down in a tangle of skis, poles, arms and legs. It was then that I noticed that as we struggled, we were slipping inexorably toward what looked from my perspective to be a 1000 foot drop off. Maybe it wasn't quite that high, but I had no intention of finding out. I struggled to get up, but slid even farther down, taking the poor Japanese gentleman with me. By now, our heads were pressed together upside down and all I could see was snow, slipping past my nose and accelerating by the second. Naoki had been silent until then, but just before someone tossed us a rope, he whispered in my ear, "Sensei, sayonara."

Of course we survived that day, and the next; in fact for the next 32 years, Naoki has been a vital part of my life, as pastor to my children, teacher to my wife and to me, comforter in a time of deepest sorrow, and friend. Now at 82 years old, one would think that he would be more interested in a cup of green tea and a nice view, but that is not who he is. Skip over to the Epilogue to see where God has taken this remarkable man. But then come back to the first chapter and discover as I have a story of courage and commitment such as few people have ever displayed. The title of this book is *Sacrificed*, and the double meaning is by intention. Naoki's story began in a time when even children were expected to give their lives for the emperor. He was no exception in that respect, but God pulled the young man from certain death and made him an exceptional sacrifice, not for the sake of an empire, but for the sake of His Own Kingdom. I am a better man for having known him, and it is my hope and prayer that the story of his life will be a blessing to all who read it.

The words which follow in this book are mine, and my wife Marsha's. But the story is Naoki's. As we sat together over gallons of coffee, he shared with us in his own language the events you will read about here. We have put them into our own native tongue, and in the process may have taken a bit of license where specific details have been forgotten or lost. But the story is true, and it is Naoki's story: a man who has truly been a living sacrifice for God.

Tony Woods

Table of Contents

Chapter 1

First Encounter

As the sun burst over the crest of Mount Goro to the east, Naoki Noguchi watched the clouds change from dark blue to deep red, then gradually fade to white. The effect was reminiscent of the Imperial Navy's flag, with its red center and sixteen rays extending in every direction. Just like the Japanese Empire itself, Naoki thought with a stab of patriotic pride.

The Meiji Restoration, beginning in the mid 1800s, had brought Japan out of its centuries-old isolation and moved it into a period of expansion not unlike that of America's "settling" of the Old West. The turn of the century brought one opportunity after another, and Japan had seized each moment, expanding its sphere of influence into the South Pacific, China, Manchuria and Korea.

But expansionist policies are rarely welcomed by neighbors, and the attack on Pearl Harbor had stirred that "Sleeping Giant"; now America, once the object of Japan's political model, had become her bitter enemy. And by late July 1945, that enemy was threatening Japan's very doors.

As the sunlight spread over Maizuru Naval Station,

Naoki peered out through camouflage netting laid over the anti-aircraft emplacement he had been assigned to supply. It was a pretty easy job so far: bringing ammunition, messages and the occasional "onigiri" (rice wrapped in seaweed) to the gunner. Not bad for a 15-year old soldier.

But all things must come to an end, he knew, and for Naoki Noguchi, it looked like it would be a race to see which ended first: his country of Japan as he knew it, or his life. The enemy was close. Word had come down the ranks that it was only a matter of time before the Allies would arrive. Already they had swept past Okinawa on their way to Japan's heartland. The Battleship Yamato, dangerously low on fuel and with no further supplies in sight, had been dispatched on a suicidal one-way mission to engage the enemy there; to purposely beach herself and provide support for the Japanese defenders; however, her task force had been spotted by American submarines, and the Yamato was sunk before reaching her goal.

But if anyone waiting along the shoreline that morning was entertaining thoughts of defeat, he dare not put them into words. While morale might have been lower than it was a few weeks ago, no one dared to think out loud what might happen. Already, so many had given their lives valiantly. Naoki could do no less.

3

He was only a boy by most standards; it was still nearly a month until his 16th birthday. But the gift of childhood was something not to be experienced by this generation. War was the only reality, and victory the only option. Just a few short months ago Naoki and his classmates at the junior high school he attended had been given the chance for true heroism: to offer their lives in the service of the Emperor. Naoki and his classmates were among the first to volunteer for pilot training, laughing together about how they would go down in a flame of glory, joining their spirits with those already enshrined at the place known as Yasukuni. "Maybe *then* the girls will appreciate us," Naoki joked. But in spite of his bravado, hope still remained for the young man, and that hope was rekindled as he watched the sun rise over Japan's Maizuru Bay.

His thoughts were interrupted by the steady drone of aircraft, rising from the nearby air base. Like angry hornets, the Mitsubishi A6M "Zeroes" formed up and headed out to sea, presumably to engage the coming enemy. Naoki stood up and waved at the brave pilots, even knowing they would not be able to see him. If only he were flying with them, perhaps on a one-way Kamikaze mission!

The planes flew out of sight over the mountains, and he settled back near his gun emplacement, halfway

4

expecting to hear the sounds of battle off in the distance. But there was no sound except for the lapping of waves along the shoreline and the occasional screech and clang of the nearby city. And then ..... a sound ..... far off in the distance. Not the wind, but something else; something man made. Something mechanical. Straining his eyes toward the morning sun, Naoki caught a glint of reflected sunlight . It had to be an approaching aircraft, he knew. And it was not alone. Gradually one speck turned into five, then a dozen, then it seemed as if the ocean itself was rising up like some huge tsunami, moving inexorably in his direction. They were coming back! Naoki felt his heart leap with joy and pride at the sight. He stood up to get a better view, and to welcome the brave warriors back to base.

But wait ..... something was wrong; the sound was different, he knew, not right. Instead of the deep, gut-wrenching roar of the Mitsubishi engines, what Naoki heard instead was a higher-pitched screaming sound, rather like the sea gulls who circled endlessly around the bay.

With a dread and growing certainty, he knew what it was, though he had never personally heard it before just now. Veterans called it the "Whistling Death", a nickname given by the Japanese for the new Allied carried-based F4U Corsair. As the aircraft approached, Naoki was able to make out the distinctive inverted gull wing design and knew with a sinking in his stomach that his Zeroes would not be coming home.

As the planes swept over the mountains to the east, they broke formation and dived in several directions. The one closest to his position cut power and started flying low and slow, around the edge of the bay close to the beach. As it passed directly in front of Naoki, he could see directly into the cockpit and almost imagine the details of the pilot's face as he scanned the rocks where he and his fellow soldiers were hiding. Some instinct kicked in, commanding Naoki not to move a muscle. Though he could not put the feeling into words, he felt like a rabbit caught out in the open, knowing he lay exposed but hoping beyond all hope that somehow the predator would not see his prey.

The moment was shattered when Naoki heard the sound of an anti-aircraft battery lighting up just to his left. Someone was trying to get the passing Corsair in his sights, and was firing rapid bursts, watching the tracers follow, then track the Corsair as it swept below them. Seemingly unperturbed, the pilot banked off to the right, exposing the plane's underbelly. In one fleeting image, Naoki could see the landing gear, folded away into the fuselage, the spare fuel tanks and the machine gun ports. The plane swung out over the bay, and for a

6

moment it looked as though he was retreating. But then it came on around, lining up directly at the source of the shooting. Opening up with his six 50 caliber Browning machine guns, he shredded the position with an almost solid curtain of lead. The gunner next to Naoki pulled back the cocking lever and swung the gun around toward the Corsair. "Stop! No! Don't fire!" Naoki yelled to the gunner. "He'll see us and kill us too!"

For the first time since the beginning of the war, reality began to sink in on the young warrior. This was no *anime*, pulled from the pages of his favorite *manga* cartoon books. There was a real man in that airplane, with a real face and a real determination to kill the enemy, including Naoki. It occurred to the young man that what he was seeing was a fellow human being, perhaps young and scared like himself, following orders not unlike those he was committed to follow.

He sank back down beside the anti-aircraft gun and noticed that his hands were shaking. As he clasped his fingers together to stop the tremor, he could feel a cold sweat seeping from his palms. As the Corsairs re-grouped and headed back over the mountain, Naoki thought long and hard about what he had experienced. What had just happened? What had brought him to this time and place? Was this the beginning of something new and exciting, and had the pages of some great adventure just been opened to him? Where and when would this all end? Would his family live to talk about these days? For that matter, would he even survive, and at what cost?

Now, nearly 70 years later, Naoki Noguchi recalls that day. The questions still surround him, but the answers have either revealed themselves over time or else lost their significance in light of the new life he has found. To fully appreciate the subsequent events which have molded and directed the man, one must go back to a time when life was simpler and joy was a part of each new day. The time: 1904; the place: Tokyo, Japan.

Think About It
First Encounter
(From Tony)

Even now, when asked about that time overlooking the beach in Maizuru Bay, Naoki Noguchi recalls with vivid clarity the event which in many ways changed his life. Many emotions went through the young man that day, but the one he remembers in greatest detail is the feeling of abject terror at the sight of seeing the face of his enemy. In that split second, war changed from a big adventure to a stark reality, with all the uncertainty and finality that only war can bring. Because of what happened that morning, ultimate questions about life and values, duty and mortality were thrust upon him, demanding answers. The process which began that day in Naoki's life is not a matter of shame, but quite the opposite: for the first time, he was able to look at his life with a new perspective, and the experience made him a better man.

Everyone can recall a "wake up" experience; or if you can't, just wait, because it's on the way. There are times in everyone's life when all that was once considered important is swept away in a moment: shattered by an impulse so demanding that it must be dealt with instantly. The impulse can usually be reduced to one single word:

9

Survive! Perhaps it's a word from a friend or spouse, or maybe a doctor. Maybe it's finally realizing that reality which you've been avoiding for so long.

Given an opportunity to transform this book from monologue to dialogue, I feel pretty sure that we could have a great exchange, comparing each other's "wake up moments".

When did you last feel afraid; I mean *really* afraid? When did *survival* surge into your synapses with such a force that it demanded your full and immediate attention? Think back to that time. What did you do? Don't be ashamed if you must admit that you did nothing. Immobility is a natural reaction, and in many cases turns out to be the best one. Just watch animals in the wild. Unless the threat of danger is unmistakable and imminent, most animals, from rabbits to deer to mountain lions will respond to potentially frightening stimulus by "freezing", making them harder to see and giving them a chance to assess the situation before deciding on a course of action. Of course in some cases, this is not necessarily the best response (see also the "deer in the headlight" syndrome), but don't be surprised or dismayed if that was your response to something really scary.

Assuming you survived your bout with reality, the important thing now is to consider how the experience changed you. In Naoki's case, it caused him to question

10

the preconceptions which had taken him to the verge of becoming a Kamikaze pilot. Just what, or more importantly *who* was that enemy he had vowed to kill? Was he in fact the bigger-than-life cartoon character he and his friends had created, then crushed, or was he instead, a human being like themselves, filled with the same fears, preconceptions and ultimate questions?

What can you do the next time you're afraid? For the child of God, the answer is simple: go to the One Who created in you the capacity for such emotion. Use that capacity in the way it was intended: for self-preservation, for self-introspection, or for both. Then look to God's Word and see what He's already told you about those moments which are sure to come your way:

...you will have success if you are careful to observe the decrees and laws that the LORD gave Moses for Israel. Be strong and courageous. Do not be afraid or discouraged.

(1 Chronicles 22:13)

The LORD is my light and my salvation – whom shall I fear? The LORD is the stronghold of my life – of whom shall I be afraid?

(Psalms 27:1)

When I am afraid, I will trust in You.

(Psalms 56:3)

In God I trust; I will not be afraid. What can man do to me?

(Psalms 56:11)

He replied, 'You of little faith, why are you so afraid?' Then He got up and rebuked the winds and the waves, and it was completely calm.

(Matthew 8:26)

Do not be afraid of those who kill the body but cannot kill the soul. Rather, be afraid of the One who can destroy both soul and body in hell.

(Matthew 10:28)

Indeed, the very hairs of your head are all numbered. Don't be afraid; you are worth more than many sparrows.

(Luke 12:7)

But Jesus said to them: 'Take courage! It is I. Don't be afraid.'

(Matthew 14:27)

12

Prayer: Lord, sometimes I'm scared. I mean *really* scared. And I don't want to feel that way. But then, I know that You created me, and You put that emotion in me. So I guess rather than ask You to make me unafraid, I should ask You what to do when I am. What can you teach me through my fears? How can these feelings help me, or protect me? How can I use my fear for Your sake, and for the sake of Your Kingdom?

I'm going to be quiet now and listen. Please speak to my heart …. And thank You.

Chapter 2

Heritage

The year 1904 was an exciting time all around the world. In that year, in New York City, the world's first underground train system, called the "Subway", was opened. Jimmy Dorsey and Glenn Miller were born, destined to usher in the era of the big bands. Dr. Seuss made his appearance as well that year, to help us remember that it's okay to say we don't like green eggs and ham, at least after we've tried them, and in London, the premier of *Peter Pan*, also known as *The Boy Who Wouldn't Grow Up*, opened to rave reviews.

But in other parts of the world there were omens lurking about which would threaten our never-ending childhood. In 1904, Japan launched a surprise attack on Russian-held Port Arthur, setting off the Russo-Japanese War. The Irish activist Roger Casement published a scathing report of Belgian atrocities in the Congo, beginning a succession of events which eventually led to his arrest, conviction and execution for treason.

Across the world in Tokyo, a baby girl was born in 1904 who would live to inspire people for the next 102 years. She was given the name Tokuko, "Virtuous Child", and one day she would become Naoki Noguchi's mother.

"Toku Chan", as her parents called her, was the second daughter of a happy family that would eventually grow to include eleven children. There must have been some longevity genes in the family, since nine of the eleven grew into adulthood (no small feat considering the time and place); and most of the children lived into their 90's and beyond; four, including Tokuko, comfortably passed the 100 year mark.

Looking back on her life in later years, Tokuko recalled happy and carefree times; one of her first memories being that of watching the funeral procession of Emperor Meiji when she was eight years old. The full significance of the passing Imperial rule was lost on the young girl, but she remembered with vivid clarity the beautiful black lacquer carriage which was pulled by a team of oxen, transporting the departed Emperor through the streets of Tokyo.

She was not naïve to the tragedies of life, though, and even many years later, could still remember the horrible images of the earthquake in Yokohama on September 1st, 1923. The quake itself was bad enough, but to make matters worse, fires broke out which destroyed most of Yokohama and large parts of Tokyo where Tokuko's family lived. Before it was over, 140,000 people had died, an event which affected a whole generation. Her father's clinic burned to the ground and he was forced to

15

return to his hometown.

It was a time for change everywhere: just six months after that disaster, recently graduated from college and barely 20 years old, Tokuko married Shigeo Noguchi, the oldest son of a family from the northern Japanese village of Yonezawa. Of course it was an arranged marriage, but since 100% of marriages at that time were arranged this way, Tokuko was happy to be relieved of the responsibility. Everyone in town placed their trust in the local 'nakodo' or matchmaker, who scoured the constituents for the best match.

Her husband was a brilliant graduate of the most prestigious university in Japan, and even better, was from a good family in Yonezawa, where her family also lived. It was considered a perfect union and the future was bright.

The Noguchi name is not particularly common in Japan, but neither is it entirely unknown, even today. Take for example Hideyo Noguchi, who was born in 1876, not far from Yonezawa. When he left home as a young man, he carved these words into the doorpost of his home, "I will not return until I make something of myself." True to his word, he became a famous doctor, and was nine times nominated for the Nobel Peace Prize, particularly for his work in discovering a vaccine for yellow fever. And by the way, his picture is on the one thousand yen note.

16

Then there was Isamu Noguchi, widely acclaimed as one of the twentieth century's most important and critically acclaimed sculptors. His Garden Museum in New York City is a place of tranquility enjoyed by thousands, and similar gardens grace nineteen other cities including Paris and Jerusalem. His work has been acclaimed as a dynamic testament to the ties between East and West.

As far as anyone knows, there is no known direct relationship between Naoki Noguchi and these men, but geographically it's possible and it seems apparent that within this broader family there is an element for which both stamina and uncommon intelligence is prevalent. We do know that Naoki was a member of the elite "Samurai" class, those indomitable warriors who ruled and protected Japan until the Meiji Restoration did away with that distinction. It was only until long after his father's death that Naoki discovered his Samurai heritage while looking through old family papers.

The same was no less true for Tokuko's husband, Shigeo. Graduating from the leading university in Tokyo, he quickly followed in the footsteps of his father, who had also committed his life to intellectual achievement, serving as a respected teacher and principal of the local school in Yonezawa. Following his marriage to Tokuko, Shigeo soon put his special gifts to work by taking on a job at a respected trading company in Osaka. There his excellent work distinguished him, earning him a promotion and a transfer to the far north island of Hokkaido.

The following year, Tokuko gave birth to a daughter; then on August 12th, 1929, Naoki was born. He obviously has no recollections of those first two years in Hokkaido, nor of the following several years when the family was transferred again back to the head office in Osaka. His father was working very hard for the company in a time when both politics and fortunes were extremely unsettled.

When Naoki was about four, it was decided that his big sister would stay back with her grandparents in Yonezawa for a while. This was not unusual in that time and place, and even in many Japanese homes today, the grandparents assume responsibility for raising the grandchildren, especially if they're living alone and there's an available little girl to 'keep them company'. There is an underlying trust within most Japanese even today for the elder generation.

For Naoki, life was good in Osaka, living with his mother and father as well as his newborn baby brother, Hideki. There was always plenty of work to do for a responsible little boy, and even more opportunity for play.

Unfortunately, those days could not continue forever

because the Great Depression was affecting even Japan. At some point, things began to fail for the family. The great fire of 1919 in Yonezawa had set the whole town on shaky ground financially, and Grandfather Noguchi's school inevitably declined and was closed, leaving him without a job. Finally he had to consider other ways of making a living. Searching for options, he decided to start up a company making the famous Yonezawa silk thread. It was a good business, but again because of changing financial climates, an insufficient market for buyers and a culture which was moving away from all things traditional, the endeavor didn't take off as expected. Instead, Grandfather Noguchi, once a man of some standing, found that all of his savings as well as his retirement money had been eaten up and there were no prospects for an upturn in the foreseeable future.

It must have been a very difficult decision, but nevertheless, the letter was written to call the "first born son" home from Osaka to take over responsibility for the family. By then Shigeo was doing quite well with the trading company, and probably on track for upper management. But family duty always took precedence in the Noguchi clan; so he was forced to resign from his job. He, Tokuko and their two young sons came back home to Yonezawa.

In spite of the difficult situation, it must have been

a joy to be reunited with the extended family. Shigeo decided to become a lawyer, as this was along the lines of what he'd been doing in the company. Unfortunately, a small town has different needs than the big city, and the demand for legal services was practically non-existent. To add insult to injury, a small town populace has even less ability to pay for such services. Before long, the entire family was on hard times.

Then one day they got a letter from an uncle who was working as a factory manager in what is now North Korea. Japan had recently solidified control of the entire area, and while potentially it could be a dangerous land because of unrest among the locals, there were more opportunities than could be counted. The uncle wrote of solid prospects for a good life and easy money in a beautiful land not unlike their own hometown of Yonezawa. After very little thought, the family of five Noguchis headed for Korea. Shigeo would be the manager of a large steel factory. Did they dare to hope for a better day?

Think About it
Heritage
(From Marsha)

Think about the idea of 'heritage' in the 21st century. Japanese maintain close ties with their ancestors, which from many respects translates as "worship". Their houses are adorned with unique furniture, built especially to accommodate family spirits, and one of the most important responsibilities a person can have is the proper care and maintenance of the family *butsudan* or god shelf. In fact, this is often a critical factor when a Japanese becomes a Christian and is called on to pray before the *butsudan*. To refuse to do so would not just be denying one's faith; it would be an unforgiveable insult to the family heritage.

People from Western cultures generally do not place so much outward significance on our ancestors, but that doesn't mean that one's family is not held in high regard.

How many of us hold our ancestors in such high esteem? We have family Bibles with generations of history carefully scrawled in by shaky hands over the years, and we often look forward to and enjoy family reunions. I say it lightly, and by no means in a religious way, but in fact we have to wonder to what extent we are the products of our ancestors, both genetically and emotionally. The things our families treasured in the past quite often are the same things we hold dear: things like integrity and honor, love and respect. Naoki Noguchi had a firm understanding of who he was, even at a young age. When his teachers spoke of duty and courage, these were not new terms to the young man. Something from deep within told him that such things were real, and a part of what made him a member of the Noguchi family. What about you? Do you have a family heritage to fall back on? Can you say in times of conflict, "This is the foundation I stand upon: a foundation which my father and his father before him built and protected with their lives. I can do no less"?

Of course for many of us, by circumstances beyond our control, such a thing is not possible. Either you have no knowledge of your family's roots, or else you have no heritage you can be proud of. When Christians talk about "God the Father", unfortunately sometimes, the image is less than ideal. Fathers fail their children, and the children suffer for it.

But it doesn't have to be that way, not for the child of God. Regardless of what your family might have been, remember that in Christ you are a new creation, with a new family and a heritage that is older than time itself.

If you can look back on your life and see loving parents and a home that was secure in its faith, then thank God for that wonderful blessing. If you can, take the time today to thank your family for the heritage you are a part of. If on the other hand, your family has left something to be desired, then pray for them; pray that God will reach into their midst and touch every life with His healing power, drawing that family together in His love and mercy. Then, thank God for the family He has given you through Jesus Christ. Look through His Word and see what a marvelous heritage is yours:

Ask the former generations and find out what their fathers learned.

(Job 8:8)

We have heard with our ears, O God; our fathers have told us what you did in their days, in days long ago.

(Psalms 44:1)

If you obey my commands, you will remain in my love, just as I have obeyed my Father's commands and remain in his love.

(John 15:10)

Jesus did not let him, but said, "Go home to your family and tell them how much the Lord has done for you, and how he has had mercy on you."

(Mark 5:19)

If anyone does not provide for his relatives, and especially for his immediate family, he has denied the faith and is worse than an unbeliever.

(1Timothy 5:8)

Prayer: Father... how interesting to call you "Father"! I mean, I know from Your Word that You created me, but I'm coming to understand that the relationship between us is so much more than that. I believe that You love me like a precious child, and that's what I want to be for You. Teach me about my family roots, Lord; show me what it means to be a Kingdom child.

I want to pray for those today who do not have loving parents to remember. Because of sin, or ignorance or tragedy, they feel like orphans, lost and alone, unloved and unwanted. Please reach out to them today. Draw them close to Your side and reveal to them just how much they mean to You. May we be real brothers and sisters today, because we both call you Father.

Noguchi Family, April 1944. Left to right: Shigeo (father), Naoki, Makiko (sister), Hideki (brother) and Tokuko (mother).

Tokuko ("Virtuous Child"), Naoki's mother

Noguchi family in 1980. Left to right: Hideki (son),
Tokuko (mother), Kazuko (wife) Makoto (son)
and Naoki.

Naoki today, Ueno train station, standing on the spot
where he bought the Bible in November, 1946

Chapter 3

Transitions

By the time Naoki was two years old, already trouble had been brewing to the west. Japan and China had long contested the area known as Korea, eyeing it as both a strategic location and as a source for raw materials to feed both countries' expanding needs. Several "incidents" had been reported since 1931, but then in 1937, four weeks before Naoki's 8th birthday, the Sino-Japanese War was declared, with Korea officially designated as part of the "Empire of Japan."

With growing conflict came greater opportunities for those who would not shy away from possible danger. Naoki's father was one such man, and when he found an opportunity to take on a management position for a Japanese-owned steel company in the northern part of Korea, he accepted it. The whole family left Yonezawa in 1943 and found a new home in what would eventually be known as North Korea.

In many ways, life was similar to that enjoyed by other colonial nations throughout history. Nearly half of all farmland in Korea was Japanese-owned by then, and over 90% of all factories. Naoki and his family lived comfortably, and he recalls those times with fondness, especially in the winter. No stranger to harsh climates after his beginnings in Hokkaido and Yonezawa, the 14-year-old found a pair of ice skates to be his ticket to new friends and endless days of fun.

School was almost a carbon copy of what he had left back in Japan, since it was maintained and taught by the "Mombusho", Japan's board of education. Naoki did well in his studies and looked forward to moving on to high school soon.

But on the war front, things were not going as well. After the attack on Pearl Harbor in 1941, new alliances had been formed, and what had begun as a Japan-China scramble for sovereignty in Korea was now a World War.

At first, Japan's powerful military and fierce dedication maintained a balance of power in their favor, but as battle lines grew more and more complex, the outcome was becoming increasingly uncertain for the Empire. More and more resources were brought into the fray, more people were conscripted to work, both from the Japanese themselves and from those under their control. So it came as no surprise when the teachers at Naoki's school took up the appeal.

"These are desperate times," Naoki's teacher announced to his class one morning. "The Great Empire of Japan is being threatened from all sides. Our military is fighting bravely, giving up their own blood so that you can enjoy the fruits of their sacrifice."

"Some soldiers have even joined the ranks of *Kamikaze*, the Divine Wind," the teacher continued with growing excitement. "Do you remember in your history books the stories of the Mongol Invasion and how the fierce warrior Kublai Khan tried to come onto Japan's shores with his army? He was turned back by the gods themselves, who blew on him and his fleet of ships with the power of the mighty *typhoon*, destroying his dream of ruling our people. In the same way, many brave soldiers have determined to give their lives, rather than let any foreign power threaten us ever again. Let me ask you, dear students: do you love your country any less? Would you be willing to go and fight, and die for our Emperor?"

Naoki was one of the first to stand up and declare his loyalty to the Empire. His friends joined him without hesitation, and in one day out of his junior high school class of fifty boys, at least forty signed up to go to war. The only notable exceptions were those who were obviously too weak to go and five Korean students, who had no interest in helping Japan to become greater.

Naoki's mother and father wept when they heard the news that evening. Tokuko cried, "But he's only a child! How could he do such a thing?"

His father Shigeo also felt his heart shattering, but in

typical Japanese fashion was more stoic. "How could he *not* do such a thing?" he asked. "Our country is facing a great crisis. Only by such dedication can we hope to survive. We must let him go, we owe it to our nation."

And so, after barely a year in his new home, Naoki left his family and joined Japan's Naval Air Force.

As with any 15-year-old, questions and doubts plagued his decision, but unlike most boys his age, his questions carried far deeper consequences. Would he be able to live up to his teacher's expectations of him? Could he also be like those brave Kamikaze pilots who threw all else aside, even their own lives, for the sake of the Emperor? But for Naoki, it was not so much a time of introspection as it was a time of great adventure. His junior high school uniform had been replaced with a military one. He had his friends around him. The days ahead promised adventures like never before. Life was good.

Think About It
Transitions
(From Tony)

For most of us, the idea of a 15-year-old boy dropping out of junior high school to become a soldier is incomprehensible. Naoki was still a child, after all, and children are not supposed to fight wars. But in fact, they do. One has only to look at the history books and even in today's newspaper to understand that kids can and do find themselves in life and death struggles all the time. From the jungles of Vietnam to the plains of Africa, "child soldiers" have been one of the saddest commentaries in human history. In some cases, such atrocities come about because of evil adults who steal children and force them into such roles. Other times, desperate times have called for desperate measures, and many a battle has been lost or won because of children who quite literally put their lives on the line for a cause.

But think about the case of Naoki Noguchi. Yes, it *was* a desperate time in the life of the nation, and if the war had not ended before Allied soldiers set foot on Japan's homeland, there is no doubt that countless women and children would have fought to the death regardless of age.

But on the day Naoki made his decision to enlist, what

31

factors led him to stand up and be counted? No one was holding a gun to his head, and so far at least, the enemy was still out of sight.

Ask him that question now, and he will tell you that two huge forces were at work that day: the strength of his teachers and the power of his peers. In Japanese society, the "Sensei" (teacher) commands great respect in just about any group. By definition, missionaries in Japan today are considered teachers, so they are almost always treated with the utmost respect, even if the people they relate to do not accept the Gospel message which is being presented. As such a missionary, I was once quite surprised at a Japanese high school where I taught for a few years. We were discussing (I thought) an issue which was controversial, and so I asked the class, "What do you think about this?" There was an uncomfortable silence, and when I finally demanded a response from one of my brighter students, she whispered, "You're the Sensei; you're supposed to *tell* us what we think!"

So it should come as no surprise that Naoki was quick to commit his life when his teacher asked it of him. The Sensei knew best; that was all that one needed to know. Whether the lesson is about math, science or dying for one's country, the Sensei will tell us what to think, and we will trust his answers to be correct.

But in addition, Naoki was a part of one of the most

important groups of all: the "nakamas": his close friends. They played together, worked and studied together; if necessary, they would gladly die together. When one announced his intention to enlist in the Air Force, they all announced their intention to do the same. This was life, and it was good.

What authority stands above you, guiding your way through the pitfalls of life? Who can you trust for wisdom in the same way that Naoki trusted his teachers at school? For some, parents fill that role, although there will inevitably come a time of questioning that will test not only a parent's trustworthiness but perhaps the parent's sanity as well. Whatever your experience has been with school, it remains a statistical fact that teachers are usually one of the most significant influences on a young person's life. A great weight of responsibility has been placed upon the shoulders of those who teach our children to read and write; may we lift them up in prayer daily.

What about the role of your closest friends? Do they help you make the tough decisions? Have they ever steered you wrong? Think back to the dynamics among your circle of friends: does one person usually take the lead in making decisions? What happens when everyone does not agree with the leader's choice? In Naoki's case, the group decided to enlist, and the group enlisted. In this particular incident, the decision was God-directed, as we'll read later, since taking the boys out of Korea was probably the safest thing that could have happened. But the key there was the *God directed* factor. If you are going to be led by any authority, be they teachers or close friends, it's a good idea to make sure that authority can be trusted. Your life may depend on it.

Look through God's Word, and see what He says about authority. Pray for wisdom in the face of uncertainty. Make good choices.

Honor your father and your mother, so that you may live long in the land the LORD your God is giving you.

(Exodus 20:12)

Everyone must submit himself to the governing authorities, for there is no authority except that which God has established. The authorities that exist have been established by God.

(Romans 13:1)

But Peter and John replied, 'Judge for yourselves whether it is right in God's sight to obey you rather than God.'

(Acts 4:19)

34

Obey your leaders and submit to their authority. They keep watch over you as men who must give an account. Obey them so that their work will be a joy, not a burden, for that would be of no advantage to you.

(Hebrews 13:17)

Submit yourselves for the Lord's sake to every authority instituted among men: whether to the king, as the supreme authority.

(1Peter 2:13)

Then Jesus came to them and said, 'All authority in heaven and on earth has been given to me.'

(Matthew 28:18)

Prayer: Lord, I want to confess to you today that I'm in a constant struggle for authority ... not *with* authority, but *for* it. I want to be my own boss, to make my own decisions, to call my own shots. I've been that way since I was old enough to look my mother in the eye and say "No!" Somehow, I just always seem to think that I can decide what's best for me better than anyone else; even You, Lord. And for that, I am truly sorry. I read through Your Word, and I know, clear to the bottom of my sinful heart, that You are my Creator, and my Lord, and my Master. Only You know me perfectly, and only You could possibly know what's best for me. Thank You for reminding me of that fact today. Help me live my life today in submission to Your authority. And when any power tries to take the place of that authority, be it society, friends or even from within myself, remind me to check with You first.

Chapter 4

Boot Camp

By the time Naoki and his friends arrived at Miho Naval Base to commence military training, some of the glitter had fallen off his original decision. Sure, everyone had admired his new uniform back home in Korea, but around here, practically *everyone* had a uniform; and most of them had a lot more decorations than his.

Sleeping accommodations left a little to be desired as well. Since this was a Naval training academy, all cadets were required to sleep in hammocks, just like they would find on a ship. As soon as Naoki got into his hammock, it closed around him like some Venus fly trap, restricting his arms and making turning over an impossibility. He noticed soon, though, that some boys were given futons, thin mattresses laid out on the floor, and when he asked about it he was told that those boys suffered from tuberculosis, and would not be able to breathe properly in a hammock. TB was rampant throughout Japan in those days, and even though Naoki never contracted it, it was always nearby. For a moment, he considered why a cadet with TB would have been permitted into the program at all, then remembered that their goal was not to thrive and survive, but to do and die, for the sake of the Homeland. For better or for worse, Naoki was here, and he would make the best of it. With every fiber of his being, he knew that he *would* make the grade.

And to insure that Naoki made the grade as a Naval Air pilot, he was placed into a squadron of trainees led by a drill sergeant who looked like he ate boys like him for breakfast. There was not an ounce of kindness on his face nor in his demeanor. But the first thing that caught Naoki's attention was the big stick that he always carried in one hand. It was known as a "Seishin Bo:" a "Character Club." It didn't take long for Naoki to know how the drill sergeant planned to use it. Every infraction of the rules, every hint of laziness or even hesitation was dealt with immediately and severely by several well-placed blows across the backside. In his unit, there would be no childishness, no personal opinions, no weakness and no doubts from those under his command. Naoki received his share of the beatings, and didn't like them any more than his classmates. But the same resilience which has been a part of the Noguchi family for generations coursed through the young man's veins as well, giving him courage and strength to endure, and even excel. He was going to be a pilot, and nothing would stop him, not even a malevolent bully with a big stick.

But it was not just the physical challenges that pushed back at Naoki. When he got his first close up look at the famous Mitsubishi A6M Zero fighter aircraft, he was amazed at the size and complexity of the machine. Back home, even automobiles were still a new commodity, reserved for the very wealthy and privileged. This Japanese-made warplane was something altogether different. From the beginning of the conflict, the Zero was the undisputed champion of the skies, with an unbelievable 12 to 1 "kill ratio" and completely comfortable on land bases and carriers alike. By 1943, Allied aircraft were beginning to catch up with better technology and defensive strategies. The F4U Corsair, for example, soon took over the field, reversing the Zero's "kill ratio". It's inverted "gull wing" design allowed for the longer landing gear necessary for accommodating the Pratt and Whitney's 13 foot, four inch three-blade propeller, but at the same time gave the plane a distinctive shape which would be forever burned within the memories of those who came against her. In response to such a challenge, the Zero became a perfect choice for the new offensive being mounted: as a one-way Kamikaze attack plane.

Naoki began studying the manuals and was soon overwhelmed at the complexity of flying. As the first seeds of doubt began to creep in, his flight instructor brushed them aside. "All you need to know is how to fly straight … straight at the enemy," he said with a glower.

But being able to fly a plane straight into combat was only a small part of the requirements of an effective Zero pilot. Even more important than the technical expertise is the *will* to complete the mission no matter what the circumstances. One of the first elements of Naoki's training took his unit to a nearby mountain. Sitting everyone down in a half circle, the drill sergeant began, "Today, our forces are battling the enemy at Iwo Jima. We are outnumbered three to one, but everyone knows we must not lose this island, since it serves as an early warning system, reporting whenever Allied bombers are headed this way." The sergeant looked out to the horizon, gripping his *Character Club* ever more tightly. "From the reports we're getting from the battle, one of the biggest advantages the enemy possesses is the M4 Sherman tank. Small arms fire, even 50 caliber machine guns cannot stop it. The only weakness seems to be on the underbelly, where the armor is thinnest. To stop the M4, a concentrated explosive charge must be placed directly underneath and detonated just at the right moment." He paused for a moment, looking each boy directly in the eye. "The only effective way to achieve such a feat is for a man to carry the explosive to the tank and place it correctly. Then at the right time, he must detonate it."

For several seconds, the only sound to be heard was the whistling of the wind around the surrounding peaks.

40

The boys did not stir or look around. When the sergeant looked at Naoki, he saw that he was looking directly back at him, unflinching. He reached down and picked up what looked like an ordinary back pack, except that it was sealed tightly with extra straps and a curious handle protruded from one side, attached to a thin rope. "This is what the explosive charge looks like," he said. "I'm going to show you how to strap it on; then we will practice running to a mock up of the M4 Sherman. You will place yourselves in the proper position underneath the tank … then you will pull the cord which sets off the explosive."

Naoki thought about what he had just been told. This was not exactly the same as flying a Mitsubishi Zero straight into the side of an aircraft carrier, but it was no less important, he knew. And if this was what the Emperor required, then this was what he would learn to do. For the next week, his unit went back to the mountain every day, strapped on simulated bomb satchels and tried different methods for getting into position under an oncoming tank. One of the most effective, albeit nerve-wracking approaches was to dig a hole in the path of the enemy, get in and pull branches over the top as camouflage. Provided the tank got to his position before the ground troops, and provided it straddled the hole properly, all one had to do what wait for the proper moment, then detonate the charge. For practice, Naoki's instructors would drive over the simulated battlefield in trucks, giving the boys an opportunity to pick the most likely path, then dig a hole in the best position. Waiting for the trucks to come, hoping they would pass over his hiding place without dropping a wheel on top of him was one of the most frightening experiences Naoki had known. But he knew it was necessary, and so did his very best to complete each training mission without mistake. He had to admit, at least to himself if not to his friends, that the exercise was scary, even knowing that everything on the training course was not real. After all, *he* was real, and one day soon he could find himself facing *real* tanks on a *real* battlefield. But whenever he or his classmates would begin to doubt, someone would crack a joke, or sing some stupid song while he danced merrily up to his target. This usually resulted in a beating from the sergeant, but it was worth it to get their minds away from the reality of what they were training for. One day the sergeant came with updated orders which only added to the hilarity. "This has just come down from the top," he began. "The Supreme Commanders have now decided that, if you are certain that your explosive will effectively destroy its target, you have permission to unbuckle the satchel and throw it, rather than keep it in place during the entire course of the mission."

Instead of the looks of relief he expected, the sergeant

was amazed to see expressions of amusement. Naoki began by stepping out in front of the group, holding up one hand in mock surrender while struggling with the buckles on his back pack with the other. "*Sumimasen* ... excuse me, Mr. Enemy san. Wait a moment while I ... get this ... thing undone." All the boys burst into laughter, and the sergeant raised his stick. But Naoki stopped him and asked quietly, "How long is the fuse on a real explosive device, sir? Two seconds? Three seconds? Just how far away can I be before I have to pull the cord, throw it at the target, then run for cover?" He looked around at the other boys, who were considering his words, then back at the sergeant. "Thank you sir, for that valuable information from Supreme Command. Please be assured that all of us will do what is proper at the time."

Besides the tank course, Naoki and his friends went through signals training. First was semaphore, using two flags to communicate at long distances. The Japanese language is usually written in Chinese characters called *kanji*. But for semaphore, this was not practical. Instead, they used the flags to simulate *kana* or the phonetic alphabet. It was great fun, and certainly less stressful than running under tanks with bombs. After only a few days of this, they were then introduced to Morse Code, with its combinations of long and short signals.

Instead of the familiar A B Cs of traditional Morse Code, however, the Japanese used what is called the "Wabun Method," so that the dots and dashes represent not letters in the English alphabet but the Japanese phonetic symbols, "ah, ii, uu, eh, oo" and so on. This method was employed throughout the war, and in fact was used to signal Japan's attack on Pearl Harbor with the message, "Niitaka Yama Nobore:" "Climb Mount Niitaka."

Naoki picked up the fundamentals quickly, and was soon transcribing messages as fast as they were sent, listening intently through headphones. As he wrote with one hand, he would tap out the message with the other, trying to get the hang of sending code as quickly as he could receive it. Asking his instructor one day when they would begin training in sending, he was told, "Oh, very soon. Very soon." But in fact, the program Naoki and his friends were a part of had no intention of ever teaching the sending part of Morse Code. Such a thing would have been a waste of time, it was decided. For the most part, Kamikaze pilots would have no need for communicating back to headquarters, and what messages they would receive would be very limited at best. During "Kaiten" training, for example, Naoki would be taught how to pilot a torpedo. Strapped into a small seat and bolted in securely, his only communication with the outside world would be a simple Morse Code

44

receiver. The only message he would hear would be one click for "Steer left," or two clicks for "Steer Right." No more was needed, or expected.

Think About It
Boot Camp
(By Tony)

Naoki's drill instructor watched his boys very carefully as he described the process of strapping on an explosive satchel, crawling under a tank and blowing it up. Sacrifice does not come naturally in most situations; in fact it is usually vetoed right away by one's sense of self-preservation. Accepting the concept of sacrifice, giving of yourself for the sake of someone or something else, is a mark of maturity, but even that has its limits. I might eventually be persuaded to share my candy bar, but give up my life? No way.

Books, movies and even history itself give us plenty of examples of men and women who sacrificed their lives for a greater cause. Think of the bodyguard who throws himself in front of the assassin's bullet, or the mother who pushes her child away from the oncoming car, or the soldier who mans the rearguard machine gun until the last of his comrades have safely withdrawn. These are heroes, and given the chance, we will honor them and tell their stories around the campfire.

But in most of these cases, the act of sacrifice is often a last-ditch impulse. After everything else has been tried, and the situation is hopeless, then that very special

46

person steps up to be counted. What made Naoki and his classmates unique in our eyes is the fact that they made the intentional decision to sacrifice their lives, long before the moment of impulse arrived. They trained for it, they talked about it, and they relished the day when at last they could prove their courage and dedication for the cause which was greater than they themselves.

Look around you today. What is worth your life? Is there anything or anyone for which you would willingly die? I'd like to think that I would not hesitate to say "yes" to that question, at least when I consider my wife and children; but at the end of the day, we simply cannot know if we will be able to overcome that power of self-preservation which resides within us.

How awesome then, when we read about Jesus, Who decided even before time began that He would shed His Godhood to take on Manhood for our sakes; that He would knowingly and willingly devote His life in preparation for that one act of supreme sacrifice, so that we might live. Look through His Word today, and find a reason for living beyond yourself. Be a "living sacrifice", taking a lifetime to be poured out for the sake the One Who gave His life for you.

He was oppressed and afflicted, yet he did not open his mouth; he was led like a lamb to the slaughter, and as a sheep before her shearers is silent, so he did not open his mouth.

(Isaiah 53:7)

Be imitators of God, therefore, as dearly loved children and live a life of love, just as Christ loved us and gave himself up for us as a fragrant offering and sacrifice to God.

(Ephesians 5:1-2)

...because by one sacrifice he has made perfect forever those who are being made holy.

(Hebrews 10:14)

He is the atoning sacrifice for our sins, and not only for ours but also for the sins of the whole world.

(1 John 2:2)

This is love: not that we loved God, but that he loved us and sent his Son as an atoning sacrifice for our sins.

(1 John 4:10)

Prayer: Lord I can't hide it: I am one selfish person. I'm always looking out for my own interests first, and I confess: even during those times when I seem to be so altruistic, I'm thinking to myself, "What's in this for me?" But You tell me that I was made in Your image, and I think that means that, just like You, I too have the capacity for love and good, and yes, even for sacrifice. Teach me how to live like You, Father. May Your Spirit guide me today in everything I do, so that I might honor You with my thoughts, and my actions.

Chapter 5

Destruction

Tuesday night, July 31st, 1945. Naoki woke from a fitful sleep. It was never easy, sleeping in a large room full of soldier-filled hammocks, but eventually he learned how to filter out the sounds. But now something new crept into his senses: a different sound. His first thought was of an impending earthquake, not uncommon throughout Japan. While sometimes coming in sudden ground shifts, pushing everything and every person violently from side to side, earthquakes can also begin with a deep-sounding tremor, advance warning of the violence to come. Naoki had experienced both, but what he was sensing now was not the same.

Soon the far away whine of an air raid siren spooled up, and Naoki knew that what he was hearing was the sound of something more terrifying and potentially more destructive than any earthquake he had felt before. On that night, several American squadrons, totaling over 80 B-24 Liberator bombers, swept over the surrounding area. Their intent was to knock out Japan's military capabilities, but the most effective way to accomplish that was by a method known as "carpet bombing". Entire mapped grids had been designated target zones, and every square foot within each grid was blanketed with incendiary bombs. On that one night, all around where Noguchi had been sleeping, wave after wave of bombs pounded the Sasebo naval base as well as the nearby towns of Miho, Yakishima and Nagasaki. At the same time, A-26s and B-25s bombed the Kanoya and Miyazaki airfields while P-51s attacked flak positions all along the northwest and west coasts. For the rest of the night, P-61s and P-51s returned to harass the area with strafing runs until Naoki thought he would go insane from the constant cacophony.

When daylight at last returned, the planes disappeared, and Naoki made his way to a high place along the cliff where he could see the area. Smoke was everywhere, and in places he could still see flames shooting up from fuel storage depots and large wooden structures. The airfield was a shambles; huge craters pocked the runways, and in places he could see the remains of airplanes unlucky enough to be caught out in the open. Down in the water, he could see two ships burning, one of them listing heavily to starboard. He wondered how many others had sunk in the darkness.

For the rest of the day, the boys were put to work cleaning up rubble, insuring that bunkers were still intact, and assessing their defensive positions. The arrival of the Liberators without warning was grim proof of what everyone had feared but dare not put into words: Okinawa was lost, and with it the outlying spotters and radio stations.

By evening, an officer came and gathered everyone together. "After last night," he began, "we cannot pretend that the enemy is not close. They are very close, and they will be here soon. What we must do is strengthen our defensive positions and do everything possible to protect our weapons." The officer looked over the group, and Naoki saw something in his face that he could not describe. Was it fear or determination? "Boys," he went on, "I know you came here to learn to fly, but I have to tell you, we have no more airplanes." Naoki felt his stomach sink in shock, and looking around at his friends knew they were feeling the same thing.

"But don't be discouraged," the officer continued. "All is not lost. We still have torpedoes, and since last year, a program has been underway to re-outfit these with manned capability. The program is called *Kaiten: "Changing Fate."* Beginning tomorrow, you will begin training. Rest well tonight!"

But rest would not come that night. A torpedo! That was certainly not the image he had in mind when he first enlisted in the Imperial Air Force. He had always pictured himself flying a bomb-laden Zero straight to the enemy, but the thought of being locked into the dark and

52

silent confines of a torpedo did not come so easily.

But by morning, his doubts had been pushed aside, and he and his fellow trainees gathered at the nearby dock where an officer stood waiting. "Boys," he said, "this is the type 10, "Long Lance" torpedo. As you will see, the pneumatic gyroscope has been relocated to make space for you, the pilot. The forward steering planes have been enlarged so that you will have absolute control over it. You will be in contact with an overhead spotter, who will guide you to your target by Morse Code: one click for steer left, two clicks for steer right."

In spite of the instructor's assurances, the Kaiten torpedo was not quite as simple as Naoki had been told. Problems persisted throughout the program with water leaks into the pilot's compartment, as well as oxygen malfunctions, so that many a pilot either drowned or suffocated long before he reached his target. When diving, the torpedo's engine often seized up, forcing it to the bottom of the ocean along with the hapless pilot. At least 15 pilots died in practice, including Hiroshi Kuroki, one of the original designers. Altogether, 106 Kaiten pilots lost their lives, with only two ships and one landing craft reported sunk by their efforts. In fact, according to post war reports, the original Long Lance torpedo, from which the Kaiten was developed, was much more effective as a "point and shoot" weapon than it was as a piloted device.

But be that as it may, Naoki and his friends were granted several days of almost carefree distraction, as they trained in the bay. The first generation of the Kaiten was built with a hatch which was removable from the inside, and would allow the pilots to jump out and swim away once he was certain his torpedo would reach its target. Later developments acknowledged that such a system was unworkable, with insurmountable problems associated with the unlocking mechanism, coupled with battle reports which concluded that not a single Kaiten pilot had ever attempted to escape his torpedo before impact. So, it remains a mystery, albeit a godsend that in those last days before the war ended, Naoki and his friends practiced on the early models, learning how to open the hatch and jump out of the speeding torpedo. To this day, Naoki laughs about the absurdity of the training. "As if we would have a place to go," he chuckles.

Besides learning to drive a torpedo, Naoki was also given the task of hiding one. Several older men had been conscripted from the area, and each trainee was assigned a group to be responsible for. "This bay will be your last line of defense," Naoki was told. "Your Kaiten will be hidden in a tunnel you have built, to be brought out and used when the enemy is at the gate."

Naoki found it strange as a 15-year-old to be in charge

of his own work crew, all of them at least three times his age. Some of his friends saw it as an opportunity to dish back some of what they had been getting over the last several weeks, and searched around to find their own "Character Clubs". But Naoki could not convince himself to become the kind of harsh task master he himself had been suffering under. These were men, after all, fellow countrymen who knew the desperate times they were in as well as he did. Besides, he thought, if we do survive these days, and I find myself around these guys, they will certainly want to treat me in the same way I've been treating them.

Work on his own personal tunnel went well, and within a few short days a Kaiten was towed inside and prepared for deployment. His instructor placed his hand on Naoki's shoulder, and for the first time, he thought he actually sensed a hint of kindness. "Next week, young man … next week you get your assignment."

Naoki swallowed before mumbling something like "Thank you," then turned back to look at the torpedo floating at his feet. So it all came down to this, he thought, trying to ignore the lump in his throat. Everything I've trained for; everything I said I would do for my country … next week.

But next week never came: at least not in the way anyone anticipated. Two days later, August 6th, on a sunny Monday morning at 8:00 am, the first of two atomic bombs was dropped on Japan, this one over Hiroshima. The destruction was so complete and so unthinkable; it took two days before Japan's government could finally realize what had happened. Then on August 9th the second one fell, this time on Nagasaki. On August 15th, Emperor Hirohito announced Japan's complete and unconditional surrender, saying in a prepared statement that, "the enemy now possesses a new and terrible weapon with the power to destroy many innocent lives and do incalculable damage. Should we continue to fight, not only would it result in an ultimate collapse and obliteration of the Japanese nation, but also it would lead to the total extinction of human civilization."

Think About It
Destruction
(From Tony)

As the old saying goes, one thing we can be sure of is the fact that we can't be sure of anything. Naoki left his home to fly a plane and to "go down in a flame of glory." Before he knew it, he was practicing so that he could run under an oncoming tank and blow himself up. Then he found himself driving a torpedo around with the promise that "next week" he would have the chance to drive one right into an enemy ship.

And then it was over; every scenario he thought might happen never did. In the space of four months, Naoki went from innocent school boy to Kamikaze in training, and then to being a defeated soldier. Ask Naoki today about change, and he will tell you it's a part of life. It's as certain as, well … as uncertainty.

How do you deal with changes in your life? What did you hope to become a few years ago? How did that work out? Does the prospect of change excite you, or drive you to despair? Part of what makes us God's creation is the element of surprise. The author and theologian C. S. Lewis often talked about being "surprised by joy," and reminded us that God is not One to be Understood, not completely. Rather, we are required to put our trust in

57

Him, and moved boldly into the future, not knowing what waits tomorrow, but knowing instead *Who* waits there.

In this world of perpetual transformation, how important it is that we keep our focus on the One Truth Who does not change. Take comfort in that unalterable fact. Be free to discover the life He has given you: try doors, sample new things. But never lose track of the God Who gave you the freedom to do those things. Enjoy the variety which is life ... while resting upon the Rock that will never be moved.

I the LORD do not change.

(Malachi 3:6)

Jesus Christ is the same yesterday and today and forever.

(Hebrews 13:8)

Prayer: Father, I confess that sometimes I think about the future, and it scares me. What's going to happen to me tomorrow? What will I be like in five years? Or ten? Lord, I rejoice in Your promise that You will always be there for me; to hold me, to guide me, to help me through whatever the future may hold. I think that I am growing daily, hopefully becoming more of what You created me to be. Thank you for that gift of progress: to know that I am not what I used to be, but by Your grace, I'm not yet what I will become. Praise You for that.

Chapter 6

War's End

It took nearly a week after Nagasaki for everyone in Naoki's camp to realize that the war was well and truly over. At first, he got up every morning at the same time, dressed in his uniform and made his way to the docks, where the boys had been training on the Kaiten torpedo. But instead of finding his instructor waiting, he saw only chaos. Debris still remained from the July 31st bombing raid, and even along the shore where they had picked everything up the day before, the tides had brought in more to take its place. Most of the officers had disappeared, presumably to meet with the generals to decide on the next course of action.

And what "course of action" would that be? Naoki wondered. Until now, there had been no talk of surrender. Even if the situation seemed totally hopeless, his orders still stood: fight and die, to the last man if necessary. Why was that different now? Rumors had been flying fast and furious, saying that Hiroshima and Nagasaki had been totally obliterated by some new kind of weapon, but surely that would be all the more reason to fight even harder! There was even talk of how to defend against this new menace. Apparently it killed by heat, and so everyone was advised to keep heavy winter coats handy, in order to protect them from the blast. Someone else pointed out that a new material called *aluminum* was being developed, and that it would turn back the power of the new weapon like an umbrella in the rain. The homeland was being threatened. If Naoki and those like him did not step up to defend his family, then who would? Why wouldn't someone come and tell them what to do?

Finally, someone did. One morning as the boys were dressing for the day's duties, a lieutenant came into the barracks. His face was set like flint, and he clutched a long *katana* sword in one hand. At first, Naoki thought they had been guilty of some grave infraction and were about to be punished severely. Instead, the lieutenant stood silent for a moment, then slowly drew his sword from it scabbard. Every eye in the room watched the blade as it reflected the sunlight streaming in from the east window. The officer studied the blade as well, gripping the handle in both hands. Naoki noticed that his hands were shaking, and sweat was running off the end of his nose.

Turning swiftly, the officer swung the sword as hard as he could, embedding the blade deep into a wooden support pole near a line of hammocks. It looked as though the blade might break, but instead the officer pulled it back out and hit the pole again, and again, and again. Finally, his rage seeming to settle, he looked at no one in particular and said, "The war is over."

The silence was palpable, no one wanting to be the first to speak up. The lieutenant repeated, "The war is over. The Emperor himself announced it. Japan has declared unconditional surrender to our enemies."

"Sir," Naoki began hesitantly. "What are we to do?"

"Go home."

"But ..."

"Go home. Everyone is to return to his hometown and wait for further orders. Report to the supply building at once; you will be given food, a blanket and whatever else is available." Without another word, the lieutenant turned and walked stiffly from the room.

Naoki was stunned. Just like that? Leave the base and go ... where? Surely not back to Korea, where he had left his family. No, of course not. He had said *hometown*. That would be Yonezawa. But what did that mean? Was he still a soldier? What would he do when he got to Yonezawa?

By now, some of the other boys had begun to stir, and were talking softly among themselves. One of his friends came closer and said, "I live in Yamagata, near your home town. Let's travel together."

Naoki stood quietly for a moment before nodding.

With hardly a word spoken in the barracks, they finished dressing, then moved with the others down the hill to the supply depot. The full impact of what they were doing that day would not be completely grasped until much later, if at all. At least one aspect of the day would never be considered for all its poignancy, not until Naoki was reminded of it years later. On that day as these boys-become-men gathered their belongings and started for home, Naoki had just passed what many young men today would consider a milestone of a lifetime: today was his birthday. Today Naoki was 16 years old.

After spending the morning at the supply depot, Naoki and his friends packed up what few possessions they had, said goodbye to all the rest in the barracks and made their way to the gate. They expected a big process before they were allowed to leave, but the guard at the gate just waved them through.

Arriving at the train station, they were surprised to see that trains were still operating, in spite of severe bomb damage all around. In fact many rail lines were closed, especially any going south toward Hiroshima or Nagasaki. Rumors were still rampant, and even though Naoki could not believe what he was hearing about some kind of new weapon, he knew in his heart that something horrible had happened; something so staggering that the Emperor himself had announced unconditional surrender. It had been the first time in history that the Emperor's voice had been heard by commoners.

But whatever was going on, his uniform still got him and his friend on the train. Soldiers were supposed to ride free, and war or not, they were apparently still soldiers. The journey took three days, traveling up the west side of Japan so as to avoid the biggest population centers, where most of the track damage was. Even in the relatively small towns along the Japan Sea, Naoki was shocked to see that here as well, the enemy's attacks had been felt. Several times, the train was diverted around bombed out bridges, and once they were even forced to disembark and walk several miles past rubble to the place where the track picked up again. Naoki and his friends passed the time talking about home and family. Surprisingly, they didn't discuss the training they had been going through. There would be a time for that later, but not now. *Next week*, the instructor had told him. If things had gone as planned, he might be slipping into his own personal Kaiten today, getting ready for a one way trip to glory. Maybe it would be better not to think about that now.

Arriving in Yonezawa, Naoki was relieved to see that there was no damage evident. I guess us country people are of no interest to the enemy, he thought with a smile. Things had not changed much, since he and his family had left, barely a year ago, although it seemed like a lifetime. Some of the markets were closed, and even the ones which were open didn't seem to have much for sale. The rice fields were beginning to turn brown, though: a sure sign of the coming harvest. At least we won't starve.

Naoki's uncle was also a soldier, serving in the Philippines. He would not be coming back for several months yet, but his home was near the train station. Stepping up to the *genkan* or entryway, Naoki slid the door open and called out *gomenkudasai*! "Anyone home?"

It was quiet for a few moments, and he was beginning to think that everyone was out. But then there was a shuffling sound, and his aunt appeared around the corner. Before he could say anything, she fell to her knees and wept with joy. "Naoki! You made it! It's so good to see you. Come in! Come in!"

Naoki slipped off his shoes and stepped up into the house. Suddenly he felt a little self-conscious in his uniform. The last time he was here, he was only a boy. And now ... and now.....

"We were told to come back to our home towns. I hope you don't mind ..."

"Oh no! Of course not! You may stay as long as you like. Put your things in the room over by the kitchen.

Your uncle is still away, but your cousin is here. Oh, it will be wonderful to have family around again."

"Thank you very much," Naoki said, perhaps a little too formally. "Of course I will help in any way I can. But," he hesitated a moment, "has there been any word from my parents? Or the others?"

Her face fell, then recovered. "No, nothing yet, but you know how difficult things are these days. I'm sure they are fine, and we'll be hearing from them soon. In the meantime, relax. I'm making your favorite for dinner tonight: white rice." With everything in short supply, most meals included only a limited amount of rice which had been diluted with anything available as filler. To have a bowl of pure rice was an almost unheard of luxury. "I'm sorry we don't have any fish to go with it, but maybe you can catch some later, neh?"

His aunt went back to the kitchen, and Naoki sat down on the tatami floor near the *butsudan*, the family "god shelf" where all their ancestors were remembered. Looking over all the knick knacks around the room, he remembered each one. Some of his earliest memories were in this house, and bringing them to mind awoke something inside him, something … comfortable. Then why was a lump forming in his throat, he wondered? This was certainly not something to cry about! Not now, after everything he had experienced.

66

But then, maybe it was precisely because of those experiences that the tears came. He would never go back to those childhood days of innocence, he knew. In fact, no one would be able to go back again, ever. The world was changing in ways that he could not imagine. Naoki could not even try to picture what the world would be like next year, or the year after that. And so, he let his eyes drift over the old familiar things in the room. It was good to be home.

Think About It
War's End
(From Marsha)

Who can imagine what went through young Naoki's mind when he was told "just go home?" *Home*, the place back in Korea where he had left his mother and father, brother and sister, was totally out of reach. That left Yonezawa, the proverbial "home town," but it was over 400 miles away; he was penniless and barely 16 years old. How he even managed the trip is a tribute to his training and maturity in the last few months before the war ended. I wonder if he 'longed' to be home or was he just a confused boy with no other options? Sometimes I wonder if we're the same way.

What if someone told you, "Just go home?" What would you do? All our lives, we've heard such expressions as, "There's no place like home," or "Home is where the heart is," and of course the classic, "Home Sweet Home." Every year in most every culture, there are set times when we are expected to be sitting at our mother's table, eating whatever it is that we remember as children while basking in her love.

For many of us the image of *home* conjures up happy memories. Naoki, even after enduring everything, both in his period of training, and then the defeat and long journey home, teared up sitting there at the family altar when he remembered the happy times he had spent in this, his home town.

The fact that the Noguchi family had suffered some hard times did not keep his child's heart from remembering all the love and acceptance that he felt in the home. Even with the war shortages, his aunt was able to shed tears of joy to see him while welcoming him into the safe and warm place, knowing that in doing so, she added another mouth to feed. I can just imagine the relief he experienced to feel welcome and safe once more.

What does the word "home" mean to you? Are you blessed to have had a rich and rewarding childhood, where you were wanted, respected and treasured? Perhaps your life has taken a different route, and if so, please accept my prayers for God's grace on you today.

I recently heard something about that famous American painter, Norman Rockwell. In his biography it was noted that his analyst, Erik Erikson, once told the artist that, "He painted his happiness, but he did not live it." Apparently, he did not have a happy home, but was instead quite unfortunate. But the artist knew how to *imagine* one, and transfer his mind's images to canvas. If you know his work, then perhaps you can remember some of the great paintings he did, the best of which depicted idealistic images of home and family.

Whether we have a happy home or just an imaginary one, we can all take comfort in the fact that our real home is in Heaven. For God's children, there is a safe place in our future: a place where all tears will be dried, and a loving Father waits to welcome us into His arms. Need reminding about what He's told us about "home?" It's always on His mind, you know. And so are you.

For this reason a man will leave his father and mother and be united to his wife, and they will become one flesh.

(Genesis 2:24)

These commandments that I give you today are to be upon your hearts. Impress them on your children. Talk about them when you sit at home and when you walk along the road, when you lie down and when you get up.

(Deuteronomy 6:6-7)

… as we have opportunity, let us do good to all people, especially to those who belong to the family of believers.

(Galatians 6:10)

For whoever does the will of my Father in heaven is my brother and sister and mother.

70

(Matthew 12:50)

If anyone does not provide for his relatives, and especially for his immediate family, he has denied the faith and is worse than an unbeliever.

(1 Timothy 5:8)

Prayer: Lord, I lift up the homeless to You today; not just the down and out people I see along the streets in town, but those who have no *real* home. I pray for those who have lost mothers and fathers, or perhaps even though the parents are still living, they are dead to their children. Most of all, I pray for every man, woman and child who does not know You as Father and Savior. They struggle through life with no hope for the great reunion You have promised Your children, when we gather together at last in Your Kingdom – our home.

Chapter 7

Last One Home

Led by a firm but gentle strength that can only be exerted in one's home town, Naoki settled into life back in Yonezawa. Eventually, his uncle returned from the Philippines, and after consultation it was decided that Naoki should move across town to his grandparent's home. Harvest time was coming, and there was plenty of work to be done. As fall turned to winter and still no news from his family, Naoki had to begin thinking about his life, and what he might be able to do on his own. The first thing that became clear was that he must finish his education. Back in Korea, he had dropped out of junior high school to join the war effort. Now he would go back. For the young man, it was one of the strangest experiences of his life. At the age of 16, he was not that much older than his classmates, but in terms of experience, they were worlds apart. Just a few short weeks previously, he had been in command of his own detachment of conscripts, assigned to build a tunnel in the rock which would hide his very own torpedo until the day came when he would lower himself inside and drive it full speed into the very jaws of the enemy. Now he was back at a desk, learning his multiplication tables and avoiding the stolen glances from the other children who sat around him.

Naoki worked hard, and soon was back on the same school schedule he had been a part of before leaving Korea. He had made some friends, and enjoyed the company of boys and girls who were not concerned with the intricacies of flying a Zero into battle, or positioning oneself in just the right place under an M4 Sherman tank so as to effectively destroy it – and yourself – in the process. Those days were seeming more and more like a dream, or sometimes like a nightmare; and except for one thing, he might have been able to put it all behind him much sooner.

That one thing was the constant apprehension for his family back in Korea. Where were they? Were they alive? Would they be coming home? Naoki would not know the answers to those questions for another year or more. Then in June, 1946, his aunt and his 20-year-old sister Makiko arrived in Yonezawa. It was wonderful to see them, but the news they had to report was less than encouraging. When bedlam had erupted, there had been no time to contact family members, nor even to return to the house. The two ladies ran immediately, stopping only long enough to cut their hair and dress like boys in an attempt to escape the pillage going on all around them. Unsure where to go to find safety, they fled in the only direction that offered a ray of hope: south, toward the 38th Parallel. Below that, the Americans had established a presence, and rumors came through that they were treating refugees with mercy; at least more so than the Russians or the Koreans. Eventually they did make their way to Pusan and on back to Japan, the first to return to Yonezawa after nearly a year of running.

By the end of that summer, Naoki finished his studies at school, and through a number of contacts was able to land a job with a chemical fertilizer company in the town of Shimonoseki far to the south, near Kita Kyushu. The company had a dormitory, and he would be assured of a place to live. No sooner had he settled into his new surroundings when word came from Yonezawa: his mother and brother had arrived home. In bits and pieces, the incredible story was slowly coming to light.

When the 15-year-old had left for war, no one could have known that in fact, he was going to the safest possible place, watched over by strict officers and bedded down behind thick bunkers. His family, on the other hand, soon found themselves in dire peril. Japan had kept a firm grip on Korea's people, but it was a tenuous hold at best. When word came of Japan's surrender, things happened so swiftly no one could possibly have prepared for the backlash to come. Russia, always lurking in the background and ready to leap at the slightest opportunity, immediately declared war on Japan, moving swiftly into Korea and taking over all they could before peace treaties could be drawn up and signed. The Korean people, never completely accepting of their colonizers, broke out in a wave of rebellion and retribution. The result was total chaos. Japanese were being killed on sight, and there was no effective authority in place to stop them. Naoki's father was at work when things fell apart, and soon found himself under the control of Russian soldiers. He may not have understood completely the language being thrown his way, but there was no mistaking the gun pointed to his head, and by their gestures knew that he was to stay on and manage the factory, at least until he was no longer of any use to them.

Back at home, Naoki's mother and 11-year-old brother Hideki saw the massacres going on in the street and knew they were in grave danger. Agonizing over the rest of her family, Tokuko grabbed whatever food and clothing they could carry and slipped out the back. By a series of miracles, they managed to work their way to a port, find a steamer headed for Japan and forced their way on board. The ship was crammed with refugees, grateful to be alive but with nothing to sustain themselves during the long trip over the Inland Sea. It seemed a certainty that mother and son would starve before landing if it were not for Hideki's "*shogi*" set, a Japanese board game rather like chess. The crew of the steamer saw the game, and asked if they could play with it. Mother said, "Of course you may borrow it ... in exchange for a bit of food."

After a long and dangerous journey, mother and son fell into the front door of her parents' house in Yonezawa, overcome with joy at seeing her sister and Makiko just arrived barely a month previously. Then, when she thought she couldn't be happier, she was told that Naoki was also alive and well, and had just left Yonezawa a few weeks ago for a job in Shimonoseki. Letters were written, and at long last, it looked like the family would be re-united. Now the only one left was Naoki's father. That story would wait several more months before finally coming to resolution.

It was late 1946, and everyone had pretty much given up hope of seeing Shigeo alive again. Then one day, a telegram came to Tokuko in Yonezawa. A man by the name of Shigeo Noguchi had been admitted to a hospital in the southern port city of Fukuoka, just a few hours by train from where Naoki was working. His condition was listed as "critical", and if there were any family members nearby, they should come at once. Tokuko managed to place a phone call to Naoki's company, and got the news to him, saying that she would be coming immediately.

It took several days and many failed attempts before Naoki finally located his father. The situation at hospitals country-wide was still chaotic at best. At last he found him, and had to stifle a scream when he first walked into the room. His father was suffering from severe malnutrition and dehydration, and to top it off had received a serious injury while on the ship which brought him from Korea. He was almost incoherent, but managed to describe how the Russians had kept him at gunpoint the entire time, forcing him to continue the operation of the steel plant, the proceeds of which were now going into Russian coffers. After almost a year, a Russian replacement had been trained, and at that point Naoki could not understand if his father had escaped or simply been let go. By now, however, his condition was deteriorating rapidly, and Naoki realized that he was watching his father's life slip away from him.

His breath coming in short gasps and his eyes half closed, Shigeo whispered, "What month is it?"

"It's November," Naoki replied, trying hard to hold back his tears.

"November .... I guess those famous Yonezawa apples are ripe by now."

"Yes ... yes they are. Would you like one, Father?"

"That would be nice," Shigeo said with the hint of a smile.

"Wait... wait here. I'll be right back." Naoki ran from the hospital room, part of him relieved to be away from death's bedside, and part of him spurred on by a ray of hope. If his father was suffering from malnutrition, then maybe an apple would help him recover! It was early, and most of the shops were still closed. He kept running, up one lane and down another, searching for any kind of fruit stand. There! At the end of a narrow street near the port, he spied a stall loaded with a variety of fruits and vegetables. Naoki glanced over the cart and saw no Yonezawa apples, but at least there were some smaller ones – Fuji's, perhaps. He didn't know, and didn't care. Slapping a coin down in front of the fruit seller, he grabbed the apple and ran for all he was worth back to the hospital. Stumbling into the room, he saw his father, lying alone in the bed, eyes open and staring at the ceiling.

"Father! Father! I've brought you an apple. You'll love it. It's not like we have back home, but I think it's good. Here try some."

Shigeo's expression didn't change, and Naoki felt a burning in his stomach. "Father! Father! I have the apple! Just try a little." Reaching up with his left hand, he forced his father's jaw down and tried to put the apple in his mouth. The more he tried, the more impossible the task became, and Naoki cried aloud, demanding that

78

his father wake up and eat. Finally, a nurse came into the room, took one look, and laid a hand across Naoki's shoulder.

"I'm sorry," she said quietly. "It was good that you were here before he passed away. So many are not this fortunate."

"But I *wasn't* here, don't you see? I left for just a moment. He wanted an apple, and I, I ....." Then Naoki did something he hadn't done in a very long time. In fact he couldn't remember the last time he had cried. Tears were not appropriate for a young man, only for children. But for Naoki, childhood had been ripped from him long ago. He could not recall a single day when he had been allowed to run and play and *be* a child. But now, he would be. No one could stop him, and indeed no one wanted to. For a long time, he let the tears flow, kneeling by his father's bedside, regretting all the years apart, all the lost opportunities, all the joy that might have been theirs if only ... if only.

Think About It
The Last One Home
(From Tony)

When was the last time you were allowed to be a child? That is not to say to be *childish*, but to be child *like*. It seems most of our lives we are being required to pull ourselves up, get a grip, grow up and act our age. Any sign of personal weakness is equated with immaturity, and that is to be avoided at all costs. For Naoki, childlikeness was never an option, even before his enlistment. Traditional Japanese homes have always been strict, and particularly for the oldest son in the family. From his earliest memories, Naoki has always seen his father as a stern disciplinarian, a man of few words and not one to be trifled with. It wasn't until much later in life that Naoki even knew of his father's pain at seeing his son go to war. Those kinds of emotions were reserved for the weak and the childish.

Standing over the bedside of the remnant which had been his father, Naoki finally gave in to the feelings which had always been in him but dare not expressed. So back to the question: are you allowed to be childlike? Not *childish* in the sense that you throw away all restraint and demand your own way in spite of whatever authority stands over you, but rather, *childlike*, knowing your

80

limitations but trusting that you will be protected and loved. This is the model our Lord has given us for our comfort and assurance: we are His children, under His authority but free to explore and discover and ... to play, certain in the knowledge of who we are. But, you may ask, am I to remain a child forever? My earthly parents, my friends, teachers, bosses and society expect me to grow up. What does God expect of me? What does a grown up child of God look like? And answer in one word: Jesus.

And Jesus grew in wisdom and stature, and in favor with God and men.

(Luke 2:52)

He went away a second time and prayed, 'My Father, if it is not possible for this cup to be taken away unless I drink it, may your will be done.'

(Matthew 26:42)

Jesus gave them this answer: 'I tell you the truth, the Son can do nothing by himself; he can do only what he sees his Father doing, because whatever the Father does the Son also does.'

(John 5:19)

81

But Jesus called the children to him and said, 'Let the little children come to me, and do not hinder them, for the kingdom of God belongs to such as these.'

(Luke 18:16)

Prayer: Heavenly Father, thank you for creating me, for loving me, and for calling me Your child. I want to be all that You created me for. Just as a child brings joy to a parent, may I bring joy to You. Help me to grow up, not that I may become independent apart from You, but just like Jesus, to be strong and obedient, fulfilling all that You have set before me to do. May I never be childish in my actions, but childlike in my faith. I love You, Lord; teach me to love You more.

Chapter 8

The Bible

Fourteen people died in the hospital that day; Shigeo Noguchi was number fourteen. His body was added to the rest and all were cremated together. When Tokuko arrived from Yonezawa and asked for her husband's ashes, there was a moment of uncomfortable silence, then an urn was produced with his name hastily scrawled on it.

Naoki and his mother left Fukuoka for home. It would be a three-day journey by train, and although most of the bombed out cities had been restored to a semblance of order, there was still much to be done. Shortages were everywhere, and the simple act of finding a meal was often the biggest challenge of the day. But on that one day as mother and son travelled back to their hometown, Naoki's search for food led to an encounter that would change his life and the lives of his family forever.

The train was passing through Tokyo, and the young man marveled as he looked out the window onto a city pulling itself up from the ashes. In some places, like the northern town of Sendai, near Yonezawa, public officials had decided to clear the rubble created by a firebomb attack and rebuild from the ground up. Even today, Sendai's wide streets and square blocks are a testimony to the foresight of engineers who were able to capitalize on a disaster and make something better in the long term. Tokyo did not have the luxury of such broad sweeping plans. As the capital city, she had to get back into business as soon as possible, and so rather than clear the debris away and rebuild, her engineers bulldozed streets around the ruins and set up shop immediately. Today Tokyo stands as one of the cleanest, well-run cities in the world, but woe be to the visitor who decides to drive around the block! More often than not, he will find himself in a maze of streets and alleyways, some leading to thoroughfares, most leading nowhere.

Stopping at Ueno Station in downtown Tokyo, where they would again transfer to a different train, there was to be a few hours delay before moving on north. Tokuko asked her son to look around the station and see if he could find anything to eat since they'd had very little for the last 3 days. The area running beside the tracks near Ueno had already become known as "Ameyoko," a new word in Japanese which meant "American Side." It was here that one could find anything from black market goods to Army surplus blankets. A friend had even written about the huge boxes of American chocolate to be had in Ameyoko, so that was undoubtedly on Naoki's mind as he jumped from the train and worked his way through the improvised market place. The smell of roasting sweet potatoes lingered in the air, and he thought that might be a good choice for him and his mother.

Walking in the direction of the delicious aromas, Naoki was about to cross the street into the heart of the market when another, almost forgotten smell hit him full on: chocolate! With an almost palpable force guiding him, he turned to his left and started down the side street. People were yelling everywhere, urging shoppers to stop and try. Scarves! Bags! Bowls! Bibles! Potatoes!

Bibles? Naoki sorted through the sounds invading his senses and focused in on the one which caught his attention. There, standing by himself, dressed in a suit in spite of the heat of the late fall day, was a man calling out in Japanese, "Modotte kure! Kami Sama ni! Mikotoba wo gorannasai! Seisho ga arimasu!" "Return to God! Look in His Word! I have Bibles!"

As Naoki edged up to get a closer look, the man gazed out over the crowd, but seemed to be speaking directly to Naoki's heart. "You've wandered too long. Come back now to the God Who loves you. Come read His Word." Almost without conscious thought, Naoki reached out and picked up one of the books, thumbing through its pages. It was a New Testament, and the Japanese words leapt out to him. However, the price for this

85

beautiful book was one yen, and that was a lot of money considering they had a funeral to host. He walked away.

Then inexplicably, Naoki returned to the table, took out his handkerchief and carefully unwrapped it, pulling out a one yen coin and slowly handing it over. One yen; the price of a meal.

The man looked at him and smiled, "This is the best purchase you're ever going to make, and because you're young, I'm going to give you this English Pocket Bible as well! Learn to read this, and you'll go a long way."

Many years later Naoki would remark, "I was looking for food for my body, but God gave me food for my soul."

His mother Tokuko was not so impressed, at least not right away, when her son came back onto the train with a book instead of lunch. Naoki explained that it would be good for him to learn English and so he had decided to buy the Bible. Sitting there with her husband's ashes on her lap, Tokuko may not have been convinced, but when reminded of the event later, as she was nearing her 100th birthday, she said, "He was the oldest son, and now with the death of his father, he was the head of the family. I would not question his decision."

It was not until much later as the train rumbled towards home that Naoki remembered that the man next to the Bible salesman had been selling chocolate.

Back in Yonezawa, the family observed all the proper

Buddhist ceremonies for laying Shigeo to rest. Then Naoki left to go back to work in Shimonoseki. As nice as it was to be back in his hometown, he was one of the few lucky ones to have a job, and it wouldn't wait forever.

As he fell back into his work schedule, he found that he enjoyed reading the Bible in his spare time, and was surprised to be gripped by a power within the words themselves. Every time he opened the Book, he seemed to discover something new, something compelling and inexplicably comforting.

One day a friend from work noticed the English Bible laying on his desk and remarked, "I didn't know you spoke English!"

"Oh, I don't," Naoki said with a grimace, "Somebody just gave it to me."

"Then you should come with me," the friend said excitedly. "I go to an English Bible study not far from here. I figured it would be good to speak English; who knows, maybe we can get better jobs! The teacher is an American missionary by the name of Elizabeth Watkins. She's very nice, and I'm sure she would welcome you. Oh! And it's free!"

Listening to his friend, Naoki felt a sensation he had never experienced before. At first he thought it was a reaction to the fact that his friend was studying under an American. Not long ago, I would have killed her, and my family would have applauded me, he thought to himself. But try as he may, Naoki just couldn't dwell on the feelings of hatred he was sure he must foster. Instead, he kept coming back to the Bible salesman's words, "You've wandered too long. It's time to come back ... come back." Whatever could that mean? He had never thought of himself as a wanderer; and just what was he supposed to be coming back *to*? Surely the man was talking about someone else ... and yet, his words seemed to ring true, in spite of his own logic.

The following week, Naoki went with his friend to see Miss Elizabeth Watkins, a Baptist missionary who taught English to a room full of boys in her home. She was kind and soft-spoken, even when Naoki struggled to learn her impossible language. Progress was slow, but he was a good student. Little by little, he began picking up the basics of English grammar, then he was able to add to his growing vocabulary list every week, usually drawn from the Bible he carried with him everywhere.

The only distinctly uncomfortable moment of the whole experience was at the end of each session, when Miss Watkins would close her book and say in Japanese, "Now boys, I want you all to know how much Jesus loves you, and wants you to follow Him as your Lord and Savior. We've been reading about all that He has done in this, His Holy Book. By His Spirit's leading, you know in your hearts what He wants you to do, and so now I must ask: is there anyone here tonight who would like to receive Jesus in his heart?"

Inevitably each week, one or two would raise their hands, Miss Watkins would pray for them and then talk about the joy of becoming a child of God. One night, Naoki looked around as she was giving her usual invitation, and realized with a shock that he was the only one who had not accepted Christ as Savior! She never looked directly at him, but he knew without a doubt that her words were for him and him alone. This was unthinkable, he thought, and waited uncomfortably until she had finished and dismissed them.

The next week's class proceeded as always, although Naoki was a little apprehensive about the invitation he knew would be coming at the end. Sure enough, Miss Watkins asked if "anyone" there tonight would like to pray to receive Jesus, and sure enough, Naoki was the only one in the group who had not done so. If anything though, the absurdity of the situation made him dig in deeper, refusing to acknowledge what she was so obviously asking for. Week after week, she invited while he sat silently. Then one night something happened that to this day Naoki cannot fully explain. As the class sat with eyes closed while the missionary lady entreated "anybody" to turn to Jesus, Naoki discovered his hand in the air. He was declaring his belief in the Lord Jesus Christ before he knew what was happening! At first, he thought it was just a case of "*ohn*", the Japanese concept of that feeling of debt one has for someone who does something for another. Maybe Naoki was just being polite and praying with Miss Watkins in order to "pay her back" for all her hard work in teaching him English. But as he began to pray the words of salvation she taught him, Naoki realized with a start that the prayer was coming not from her mouth but from his own heart. He honestly believed what he had been hearing all this time! Indeed, he had been a wanderer, straying far away from the God Who had created him, Who loved him more than anyone else, Who wanted to welcome him back home – his real home in Christ's Kingdom.

From that night, Naoki Noguchi became a new person. He still possessed all the strength of character which had brought him up as a faithful child of the Empire; but now that strength was being re-directed into the purposes for which he had been created, as a child of the Kingdom.

Think About It
The Bible
(From Tony)

In Japan, there are two greetings to be used whenever someone comes into a house. The first is *irra-shai-ma-sei*, and it means, "You are most welcome here, please come in." The second is *o-kae-ri-na-sai*, and it translates as "You've come home." The first greeting is for visitors to your house, and the second is reserved for family members, returning to their dwelling place.

The Bible teaches that, as a child of God, I am a citizen of His Kingdom. I am no longer a wanderer, peering through the window of some fine home and wishing I could go inside and enjoy its warmth and richness. I am instead a pilgrim, moving intentionally along the road which has been laid before me, not knowing exactly what lies around the next bend but absolutely certain of what lies at the end of the journey. When I come to the end of my life, I will be able to approach Heaven's gates and hear my Lord call out *"okaerinasai*, My child; you've come home!"

This is why Christians often refer to death as a "home coming." Yes, it can be a profoundly sad time for the living to have to suffer separation from friends and loved ones, but what a joy to know that they have only preceded us to that wonderful place where every tear will be dried and joy will reign forever. If you or someone you love does not know that peace and assurance today, then surely, this is the time. You've wandered too long. Come back.

Men will stagger from sea to sea and wander from north to east, searching for the word of the LORD, but they will not find it.

(Amos 8:12)

What do you think? If a man owns a hundred sheep, and one of them wanders away, will he not leave the ninety-nine on the hills and go to look for the one that wandered off? And if he finds it, I tell you the truth, he is happier about that one sheep than about the ninety-nine that did not wander off.

(Matthew 18:12-13)

Do not let your hearts be troubled. Trust in God; trust also in me. In my Father's house are many rooms; if it were not so, I would have told you. I am going there to prepare a place for you. And if I go and prepare a place for you, I will come back and take you to be with me that you also may be where I am.

(John 14:1-3)

Prayer: It's a big world out there, Lord. I admit that I've spent a lot of time exploring, sometimes in places where I knew I shouldn't be going. And all those places just never seem to take me anywhere; I'm always left with a sense of emptiness and unfulfillment. And then I realize how big Your world really is! The side streets and back alleys I've spent my life stumbling through are nothing compared to the vastness of creation. Lift my eyes, Lord; help me see all that You have in store for Your children. I don't want to wander anymore. Don't let me reach for the chocolate when what I really want is the Bible. I want to *go* somewhere that has a purpose. Send me on a mission. Use me for the sake of Your Kingdom. Guide my feet all the way through this life and beyond. And at the end of this life, may I hear those precious words, "You've come home."

Chapter 9

The Call

Following Naoki's decision to invite Jesus Christ into his life, Elizabeth Watkins invited him to church. Shimonoseki Baptist was nearby and welcomed him with open arms. The pastor of the church was a remarkable man by the name of Ozaki Shuichi. Whenever Naoki heard him speak, he was amazed at the way he could take any verse from the Bible and unfold it like a precious gift, turning it in every direction so that every facet came alive and relevant. How he could do that week after week was a mystery to the young man, who had never considered himself much of a conversationalist, much less a public speaker.

Moreover, Ozaki Sensei handled English almost like a native speaker. Whenever he and Miss Watkins spoke together, Naoki thought it was like listening to some famous Chinese opera: something to be appreciated but never to be understood. Miss Watkins explained to the discouraged young man that Ozaki Sensei had been blessed with a special gift for languages. No one knew at that time just how deep and wide the blessing went, or how some day he would be standing before thousands and translating for Dr. Billy Graham. But Miss Watkins

94

went on to explain to Naoki that all Christians received special gifts from God: gifts to be used for the work of His Kingdom.

"But what is my gift?" he asked.

"I don't know. That's something for you to discover," she smiled.

Naoki wondered about that and thought, well, at least I know what two of my gifts are *not*: English and public speaking! Instead, he decided to pour his energies into the upkeep of the church building. It was winter, and the meeting room was warmed by an old wood burning stove. Naoki would arrive at the church before anyone else, cut up a generous supply of firewood, and have the place warm and toasty by the time people arrived for worship.

One day, Ozaki Sensei came in to find the young man hard at work, cleaning out the ashes in the stove. "You're such a big help," he said. "I don't know how we ever got by without you." Embarrassed by the compliment, Naoki just smiled and kept working.

Ozaki Sensei continued, "You know, a lot of people here have commented on your hard work and dedication. I think God is really using you in this church." He hesitated. "I think He might like to use you even more."

Wiping down the stove, Naoki grinned and said, "Miss Watkins said I should discover what my spiritual gift is. I enjoy keeping the fire going; could that be my gift?"

Ozaki thought a minute, then said, "It could be. God uses His people in a variety of ways; something like this is no less important that what I do. But tell me this, Naoki-san: have you ever thought of doing what I do?"

"What you .....? Oh no, never. I'd be terrified to stand up in front of people. Do you know why I started doing this job with the stove? It's because I can come early before anyone else arrives. That way, I don't have to talk to anybody. I'm not a speaker, Sensei. I never have been, and I never will."

"Be careful what you say, Naoki. Telling God what you *won't* do is often a sure way to end up doing it. Do you remember the story of the boy learning to ride a bicycle? As he starts down the road, he sees a big telephone pole coming up. The closer he gets, the more he says to himself, "Don't hit that pole don't hit that pole don't hit that pole." What happens down the road is not exactly clear, but one thing is certain: he *will* be hitting that pole!"

They laughed together, then Ozaki Sensei continued, "Anyway, let's pray about it, shall we? We can ask God to show you what He has in mind for you. Whatever it is, I'm sure it will open up a whole new world for you."

The more Naoki prayed about God's will for his life, the more convinced he became that this was something he needed to share with his mother. He had known

96

such peace and joy since his decision, and more than anything he wanted her to know it as well. He wrote his thoughts down on paper, said a prayer and sent it to Yonezawa. A few days later when Tokuko opened the letter, she read:

Dear Mother,

Something wonderful has happened which I must share with you. I have become a Christian! I go to a wonderful church here and it's just like being in a family, where everyone loves and watches out for each other. It's the best thing that has ever happened to me. And you were there when it all started. Do you remember that day in November at Ueno Station, when I bought the Bible? I read it, then read it again, then studied it with a group of boys my own age. Now I am part of Shimonoseki Baptist Church here, and it's all so fantastic. Mother, I want you to find a church there in Yonezawa and go to it. I hope you will like it as much as I do. Naoki

Tokuko smiled to see that her son was happy, but a little concerned to read about his becoming a Christian. She did not know much about Christianity, and after all, she was Japanese. Such a thing just wasn't done. Still,

97

he was the head of the family, and if he said she must go to church, then she would go to church – at least once. Yonezawa Baptist Church was within walking distance, so the next Sunday Tokuko put on her kimono and went to their worship service. The people certainly were friendly, and the music was pleasant. She enjoyed the time, said her goodbyes and went back home. She had fulfilled her son's wishes; now she could get back to whatever it was she was doing before.

However, the following Sunday, Tokuko was awakened to the sound of a drum, beating nearby. She looked out her window and was horrified to see a group of people standing in front of her house. One man was beating on a big drum and they were all shouting, "Mrs. Noguchi! Mrs. Noguchi! Come to church again like you did last Sunday!" She was so unnerved, she got dressed and went with the crowd to church, if for nothing else to make them be quiet in front of the neighbors. After the worship service, however, she asked the pastor, Tanaka Sensei if she could have a word. Going back into his office, she explained, "You might as well know, I came last week because my son told me to. He's down in Shimonoseki and, well, he's become a Christian. He's very happy, and I'm very happy for him, but ..... I'm sure you understand."

Tanaka Sensei smiled but said nothing, so Tokuko

continued. Pulling Naoki's letter from her purse, she unfolded it and passed it across the desk. "Here's what he wrote me." Tracing down the words, she said, "Yes, here it is: "...*when it all started. Do you remember that day in November at Ueno Station, when I bought the Bible?*"

"That's when it began," Tokuko said, folding the letter back up. "He bought the Bible at Ueno Station that day, and he hasn't been the same since."

Tanaka Sensei sat motionless for a long time, then reached into his pocket and pulled out a calendar. He studied it a long time, then turned it around and pushed it across the table toward Tokuko. "Mrs. Noguchi," he began, "I can't prove what I'm about to say, except to show you this note."

Adjusting her glasses, Tokuko glanced at the calendar, then leaned forward and looked closer. Finally, she looked up at Tanaka Sensei, eyebrows raised.

"That's right, Mrs. Noguchi. I don't remember your son personally; there were so many people passing through Tokyo. But at that time, I was at Ueno Station, and I was selling Bibles."

That got Tokuko's attention. She listened very carefully to the simple message of salvation from Tanaka Sensei. She was back at church the following Sunday and the next. Before long, she was convinced. She wrote a letter to Naoki, and within a few short days, his reply came back:

Mother, I'm so happy for you. These are exciting times, and you don't know the half of it. Since I last wrote you, I have decided to quit my job and go to seminary. Can you think of me as a preacher? The church here is very supportive of my decision, and has offered a room in the basement for me to live in, since I can no longer stay at the company dormitory. There's plenty of room, and I will have much to do. I need your help. Would you consider coming to Shimonoseki and living here with me? P.S. Ozaki Sensei here says he would be honored to have you here. In fact, they are planning a baptism service very soon. I think you're on the program!

Two years later, Pastor Naoki Noguchi stepped up to the pulpit. Shimonoseki Baptist Church needed a shepherd to lead the flock, and everyone agreed that he was God's man for the job. Glancing over to Tokuko, sitting by the window in her finest kimono, he stole a quick smile. Only she knew his secret. "I still don't know if this is my gift, Mother!" he had said earlier. "How could God call someone like me to be a preacher?"

100

"How could he not?" she said with a look of wonder. "God has been preparing you for all these years. He has an investment in you, you know."

"But why am I still so nervous about it? I get sick every Sunday like clockwork! Why would God give me a gift, then make me afraid to use it?"

"Maybe you just need a reminder of what a powerful tool it is that God is letting you use. Think back to what you did just a few years ago. Why, you were ready to *die* doing your duty! And yet you did not feel then what you feel now." Tokuko leaned over and gave him a motherly pat on the cheek. "To be sacrificed for an Empire is a fine and noble thing, but nothing to be compared to a living sacrifice, completely devoted to God's Kingdom. Yours is a gift not granted to everyone. Yes, you *should* be nervous about using it. Use it well."

Think About It
The Call
(From Tony)

Discovering that there really is a God Who loves you and sent His Son Jesus to die for you is just the beginning. As Naoki soon discovered, there is more ... *so* much more. New sights and sounds, new friends, new roads and a whole new heart: these are but a few of the many facets of life as a Kingdom child. More importantly, there are gifts, and purposes for which those gifts are to be used. Discovering your gifts and putting them to use is a lifetime joy which can be summed up in one word: *Call.* God did not just put you together in His workshop then set you on a shelf to admire; He created you with a purpose in mind. Have you ever wondered, if Heaven is such a great place, as the Bible assures us it is, then why are you still here? Jesus said He was going to prepare a place for us ... is He still working on it? Listen: there is only one of two reasons why you're not having the time of your eternal life in Heaven instead of sitting there reading this book. First, it may be because "Heaven" is not yet on your ticket. Do you have the assurance that if you died before coming to the bottom of this page, that the next sight you see would be your Heavenly Father welcoming you into His Kingdom? And before you think about it, it's not going to help stopping reading before you get to the bottom of the page. If for some reason, you don't have that kind of assurance, stop what you're doing and deal with it, right now. Turn to God in your heart now and ask the simple question: "Are You there?" The Bible promises that the honest seeker will never be turned away. Ask the question, then wait for the answer.

The second possibility for the reason that you're not in Heaven right now is the fact that God is not finished with you yet. And hear me well: if you have a *pulse*, then be assured that God is not finished with you. There are still purposes to be accomplished, words to be said, things to do. Think back to what Jesus said in John 14 (see below); do you think He would hesitate an instant to bring you into the place He's prepared for you if there were nothing else standing in the way?

What is God's call for you? Are you fulfilling that call? Look at His Word and find exactly what you need, be it a word of encouragement, marching orders or maybe even a swift kick in the pants. Whatever you find, thank God that you're on speaking terms.

In my Father's house are many rooms; if it were not so, I would have told you. I am going there to prepare a place for you. And if I go and prepare a place for you, I will come back and take you to be with me that you also may be where I am.

(John 14:2-3)

All Scripture is God-breathed and is useful for teaching, rebuking, correcting and training in righteousness, so that the man of God may be thoroughly equipped for every good work.

(2 Timothy 3:16-17)

...being confident of this, that he who began a good work in you will carry it on to completion until the day of Christ Jesus.

(Philippians 1:6)

Prayer: Good question, I guess: why *am* I here, and not with You in Heaven? Lord, if there is any reason why I am not Your child today, please make that perfectly clear. I know my eternal life depends on it, and I don't want to get that wrong. But I know You love me, and I know You will not condemn me for my ignorance. Speak to my heart just now, I pray. Tell me that You love me, and have work for me to do, which is why I'm here today, and not rejoicing in Your Kingdom. Show me my call, I pray. Enable me to do the work You have set out for me to do. And then help me accomplish it. When that is finished at last, I will fall at Your feet, completely used up and ready for whatever is next.

And … thank you. Thank you.

Chapter 10

The rest of the Story

After the exciting years from the end of the war and his conversion to the One who was sacrificed for us all, Jesus Christ, Naoki was able to finish high school by attending night school, all the while holding down a full time job and supporting his family. The year was 1952.

When he finished High School, he realized that life was getting easier. Both his mother and sister, who along with his little brother had moved from Yonezawa into the church basement with him, now had full time jobs so he didn't have to work such long hours. His pastor saw this as a great opportunity, so soon he was asked by the Shimonoseki church to pray about attending the nearby Baptist Seminary of Seinan Gakkuin. The church even offered to help a little with the tuition!

1957 was an important year. He graduated from Seminary, took a job as senior pastor of Shimonoseki Baptist Church and married one of the members of the youth group, a beautiful and spirited girl named Kazuko.

He and Kazuko would work side by side for the next forty nine years until her death in 2006, and after having raised two wonderful boys, Makoto and Hiroshi.

Makoto is a teacher and has a wife and four children,

all serving the Lord in different ways

Hiroshi works in a company and also has done well. They also have two children.

When the boys were small, in 1964, the Noguchi family left Shimonoseki so that Naoki could teach with his former mentor and pastor in the newly formed part of the seminary that specialized in non-academic pastor training. We call this a 'diploma program' today. He was there until 1970.

• In 1970 they went to Tomino Baptist Church in Kitakyushyu.

• 1980 brought the Noguchis, now without the boys as they were grown, to the northern town of Sendai to start Sendai Kita Baptist Church. This church grew quickly and successfully and is where the author met Noguchi Sensei and began to learn from him. They served 13 years in this church. Then because of Kazuko's failing health (due to contracting Hepatitis C during a blood transfusion years before) they returned to the southern island of Kyushu.

• 1993-2000 saw them working in Fukuma Baptist Church.

• In 2000 Noguchi, at age 73, decided to officially retire. That lasted about two years, until he accepted a call to pastor Ashiya Baptist Church, where he served from 2002 until 2007.

- 2006 saw the sudden death of beloved Kazuko. Official cause of death was stated as heat stroke, most likely exacerbated by the Hepatitis C.
- 2007 Mother, Tokuko died peacefully at almost 103 years old.
- 2007-2009 was another interim position, this time at Wakamatsu Baptist church.
- 2009-2010 was in the far northern town of Same (A word which means "shark" and is pronounced "Sah-May)."

Then, typical of the Noguchi family, Naoki, as he was packing to move into a retirement village at age 82, declared that his "shomikigen" was not up yet (his 'use by date') so he rearranged his bag, and headed north to the suburb town of Yoshioka, near Sendai. He moved into the upstairs study of a church he and Kazuko helped resurrect with the Woods so many years ago; Yoshioka Baptist Church and kindergarten.

There you'll find him today, full of life and always smiling. Because of the great need for volunteer housing after the Great North Eastern Earthquake of March 11th, 2011 Noguchi has opened the church to house and feed people from all over the world. He invites them to share in the worship services as well as all the adventure of ministering to a country that so needs a savior.

His email address is noguchi-naoki@ac.auone-net.jp
I'm sure he'd love to hear from you!

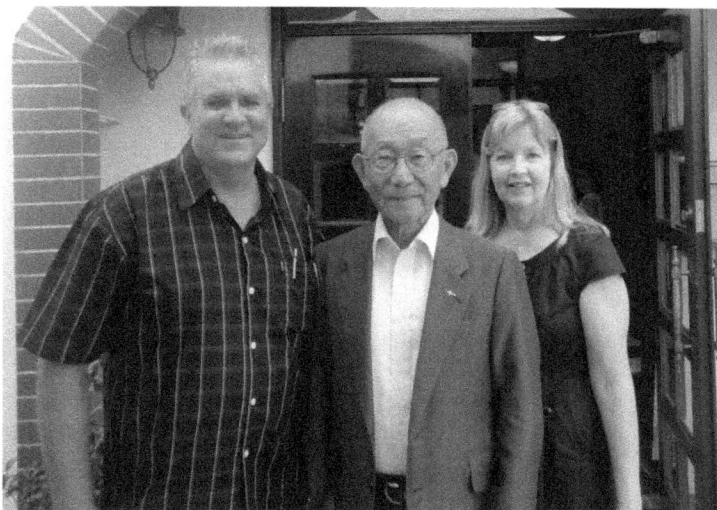

Naoki Noguchi with Tony and Marsha Woods in front of
Kita Sendai Baptist Church.

Other Marton Publishing Devotional Books

Available at martonpublishing.com

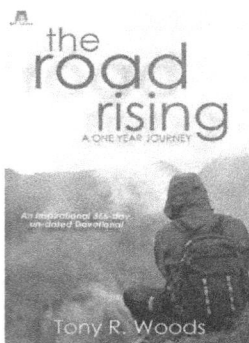

The Road Rising - Tony Woods

A one year devotional book which follows the daily journey of a man on a backpack trip. In the course of his journey he encounters fire, storm, loneliness and true friendship throughout his commitment to follow the One who called him to the challenge.

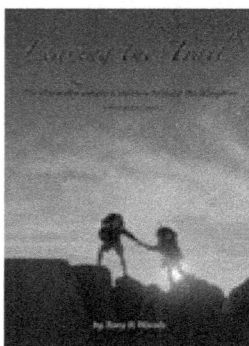

Leaving the Trail - Tony Woods

A sequel to "The Road Rising," Fisher and his young wife Sandy are told to leave the safety of the marked path and venture into the wilderness to find pilgrims who have lost their way. Can be read as a novel, a daily devotional, or as a dramatic analogy to the missionary call.

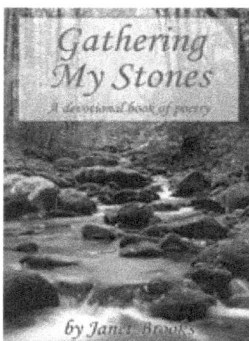

Gathering My Stones - Janet Brooks

An assortment of Bible verses and poems, for those who hold prayers within their souls, but no words to voice them; for those who desire more words of praise, more encouragement, more of God; a glimpse into what could be theirs as children of the King.

Other Marton Publishing Books

Available at martonpublishing.com

A Hope & A Furutre - Marsha N Woods
Born on the heels of the horrific Spitak Earthquake, little Ma'sha had little hope for survival, much less for any kind of joy in her future. But there was a Power over it all with a different kind of plan, from the Russian village of Armavir to a new home and a new future.

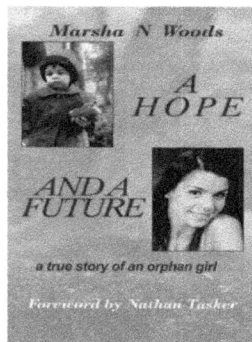

River Crossings - Marsha G Woods
Began as a daily blog from Bangkok, "River Crossings" offers in book form a close up and extremely personal account of missionary life from the viewpoint of one who has encountered and crossed the mission field's rivers for over forty years.

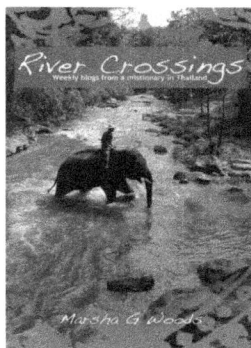

Looking for a Lamb - Tony Woods
A father's journey up the mountain of grief and beyond. In this unique analogy which reflects upon Abraham of the Bible, follow the painful ascents of two fathers. Both discover at the summit the only Lamb Who can make sense of the tragedy.

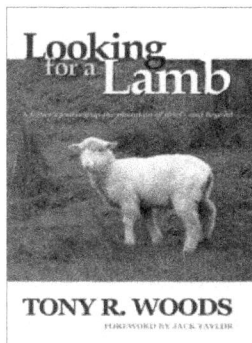

Other Marton Publishing Books
Available at martonpublishing.com

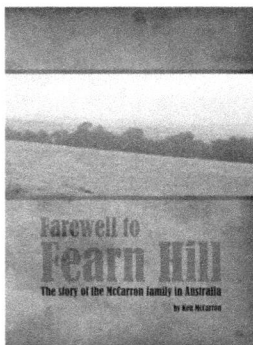

Farewell to Fern Hill - Ken McCarron

The story of the McCarron family as they leave their homeland in 17th century Scotland and begin a new life in Australia. Farewell to Fern Hill is a revealing look through one's family's record at some of the early pioneers of this last true frontier.

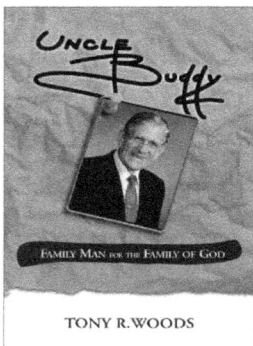

Uncle Buddy - Tony Woods

When missionary Buddy Woods' wife passed away, he felt that he would be following her soon. But God had other plans for this faithful vertern of many years of missionary work in Africa and China. Many wonderful stories through his journey of a life making a difference.

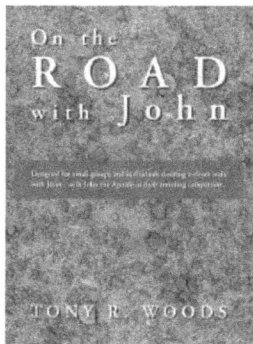

On the Road with John - Tony Woods

A one year study of John's Gospel designed especially for small groups. Each of the fifty two lessons includes a "Road" worksheet which guides the reader through analysis, contemplation and discussion of particular themes within the lesson.